P9-BZM-637

Reformed and Feminist

REFORMED AND FEMINIST

A Challenge to the Church

Johanna W. H. van Wijk–Bos

Westminster/John Knox Press
Louisville, Kentucky

Book design by Gene Harris

First edition

Published by Westminster/John Knox Press
Louisville, Kentucky

PRINTED IN THE UNITED STATES OF AMERICA

9 8 7 6 5 4 3 2 1

Library of Congress Cataloging-in-Publication Data

Van Wijk-Bos, Johanna W. H., 1940–
Reformed and feminist : a challenge to the church / Johanna W.H. van Wijk-Bos. — 1st ed.
p. cm.
Includes bibliographical references.
ISBN 0-664-25194-3

1. Feminism—Biblical teaching. 2. Feminism—Religious aspects—Presbyterian Church. 3. Women in the Bible. 4. Bible—Evidences, authority, etc.—History of doctrines—20th century. 5. Women in the Presbyterian Church. 6. Presbyterian Church—Doctrines. 7. Reformed Church—Doctrines. 8. Van Wijk-Bos, Johanna W. H., 1940– I. Title.
BS680.W7V35 1991
220.1′3′082—dc20 90-19895

In Memoriam

Gerrit Cornelis van Wijk

Johanna Martina van Wijk–van Dam

Contents

Preface and Acknowledgments

This book is written, first of all, for those of us who are, in the words of theologian Catharina Halkes, "critical, troublesome, but believing" women. If there is lot of my own experience in the book, that is because it interests me to see how I arrived where I am; I hope that it may interest others and help them examine their own roots and commitments.

One will find the basic biblical reference to be the Old Testament, or Hebrew Scripture. I have a deep concern that our congregations are losing this essential part of the Bible, a loss that I believe to be perilous for the Christian faith. The translations of the text are my own, unless it is noted otherwise.

One will not find the term "Reformed tradition" in this book. I find those words misleading, and I don't believe that any such thing as "the Reformed tradition" exists. Many streams flow from the Protestant Reformation, all of which need examination and often reform. My central concern is with the Reformers', and especially Calvin's, understanding of the place and authority of the Bible. I propose to explore whether it is possible and even helpful for Christian feminism to maintain, in some sense, Calvin's understanding of the place and function of the Bible.

This book also is written for people who have questions about their Reformed heritage and for those who wonder about feminism and its connections to Christianity. I wrote the book for people who like to ask questions and wrestle with them. Finally, I wrote in the sincere conviction that, through the Bible, God's liberating Word comes to us and provides us a vision for a new way of being.

Many people contributed on the way to the expression of the thoughts presented here, although none of them are to be held responsible for what I have said. The idea for this book arose out of a meeting of Presbyterian Christian educators in New Windsor, Maryland, in April 1987. They were the first of many groups of stimulating and responsive people who restored my confidence and enthusiasm and above all gave witness to the possibility of Christian feminism.

I thank Jennifer Lavery Miller and Karen Brau, who gave generously of their ideas, their poetry, and their laughter during the time this book was being written. To my feminist husband, David, go my thanks for providing a safe environment and a critical and supportive presence. My friend and colleague Burton Cooper I thank for his many helpful suggestions and especially for the subject and title of the first chapter. Friends and colleagues David Hester and John McClure receive my gratitude for patiently listening to the way I wrestled with the second chapter. Editors Cynthia Thompson and Walt Sutton of Westminster/John Knox Press deserve thanks for their receptivity to the idea of the book and for their suggestions during the writing of it.

In looking back to those who contributed to the book long before it came about, I recognize with deep gratitude the gifts of my teacher and friend, the late Pieter Hubrecht de Pree, who taught me the love of Scripture. Finally, the book is dedicated to my parents, who taught me the love of language and the value of self.

1

Dutch, Reformed, and Feminist

The occupation of the Netherlands by Nazi Germany began in May 1940. Many Dutch people had not believed that an occupation by their neighbor, Germany, would ever become reality. A sense of "this cannot be happening here" pervaded the first few months of the war in Holland. Another reaction to the war was the feeling that it could not last long—a few months, a year at the most. Perhaps these are common reactions of folk when they endure what cannot be endured, for they keep actual events somewhat at a distance. In any case, in spite of people's feelings, the occupation *did* happen in Holland, and it lasted. The Netherlands was not freed until May 1945; the horrors of the war and occupation were a part of people's lives for five dark years. These five years were also the first five years of my life.

Growing Up Dutch

Strange as it may seem, for a long time I did not weigh the influence of these years on my life and failed to consider them an important factor in my formation. Perhaps because of an exceptionally fortunate family environment, I always thought of my youth as a happy one. Yet not only those first five years but all of my childhood and adolescence were colored by the events of 1940–1945. A war is not over when it ends. Many of the worst aspects of Hitler's Third Reich were revealed only after the war ended. My home and school life were permeated by the effect of these revelations. My teachers in elementary and high school had been adults during the war; some of them were victims of concentration camps, and many had suffered severe personal loss. Students like myself were surrounded by the literature that had arisen from the war: poetry and prose written by victims. There were the books that adults tried to prevent youngsters from perusing because of the obscenity of the illustrations, illustrations from the destruction of the Holocaust. There were also the visible reminders of the war in ruined buildings, blackened remnants of houses and churches that stood for years. In fact, it was difficult to go anywhere or do anything and not be reminded of the war. The remembrance surrounded us in all kinds of shapes.

In my family, the remembering took shape in family stories told during gatherings at birthdays and other celebrations. In these stories, my father often played the role of the buffoon who miraculously escaped the fate of becoming a victim of the Nazis. The stories were dramatic in content, but they were not sad in tone. I remember a great deal of laughter during the tales of these escapades, tales told over and over again until their form became fixed. They were a part of the family repertoire, of the "remember when . . . ." Thus one tried to tame the beast and to a degree succeeded. The war came to be seen as an interruption in our otherwise peaceful lives. It had been dreadful, but it was over.

For inhabitants of occupied countries, the dominant factor of life was fear: fear for one's possessions, for one's daily provisions, and above all fear for one's life and the lives of those one loved. All the rules were gone. Rules of ordinary, polite behavior and rules of justice no longer operated. People could be rude without incurring disapproval; they could kill without being punished. The Germans were in charge; they could do what they wanted—the Dutch could not. This was so simply because one was either German or Dutch. There was no logic to the way things were ordered but the logic of brutality. In such a climate a child absorbs fear with its mother's milk.

Where there is fear, there is secrecy. Hiding things and activities from the enemy became people's daily business. All around me people were busy hiding their possessions, their actions, and frequently persons. Secrecy was acutely important for the Jews and those working in the Dutch Underground, but every Dutch person was, to an extent, involved in secrecy. Those who revealed secrets were betrayers. People were divided basically into two groups: "bad" people were the occupying enemy, those who collaborated with them, and the people who administered the government of the country, who "upheld the law." "Good" people were powerless; they went in fear of their lives, and they despised the group in power. Good people helped those who most needed protection. One could hardly tell one group from the other since, in the case of collaborators, nationality did not reveal alliance. Ostensibly decent people could suddenly turn and become betrayers. The outcome of the story of Anne Frank provides an example of this type of action.

In my village there lived a Jewish family also named Frank. They had been a part of the village community for a long time, certainly as far back as my grandmother's day. At a certain point, it became clear that this family had to go into hiding elsewhere. They had two children, both girls, one only a baby. In making their arrangements, the parents decided to take the older child with them but leave the baby with a family in our village for the duration of their time in hiding; it would be difficult to control a baby in a hiding place. Perhaps this decision was made for them. Who knows? No sooner had the Franks gone than the woman who had agreed to take care of the baby reported its presence to the mayor's office. The mayor was a well-known collaborator with the Nazis, and the baby girl disappeared into one of the death camps. What had occurred to change the mind of the woman who had promised to take care of this child? One can hardly assume that she accepted the task with betrayal in mind. Perhaps she became deeply afraid for herself and her family as well as for others in the village. The Nazis were known for taking reprisals against whole groups as punishment for an individual's misdoings. Perhaps she told herself that no one would harm a baby girl. Who knows? My mother had a baby girl approximately the same age as the Frank baby. She must have come home and told the news to my father. She must have looked at me, her baby girl, and wondered how she would feel if such a thing had happened to us. Perhaps she thought she should have agreed to hide the baby. But she wasn't the one who was asked. She may not have known of the arrangement. And so the littlest ones had their protection taken away from them and were delivered to the oppressor.

The child that I was absorbed the feelings—feelings of rage against the injustice, feelings of pain and compassion, feelings of helplessness in the face of overwhelming evil, and feelings of horror against those in power. The injustice and evil were, moreover, not accidental; they were built into the very structures of our lives. Systems of injustice had bred the fear, the need for secrecy, and the eventual betrayal. These systems had to be changed, and they were changed, in the Netherlands, with the liberation. But the child that grew up carried with her forever the consciousness that structural injustice brings about the worst kind of oppression and that the battle against injustice must always involve systemic change.

The Netherlands was liberated during May of 1945, when I was almost five years old. I have my own memories of this event. The general mood of those days especially remains with me. No words describe this episode better than wild jubilation. Of proverbial Dutch reticence and sedateness, no trace was visible. The Dutch flag and colors of the Royal House, until then forbidden from display, were abundantly in evidence; on flagpoles, on clothes, on houses, and in gardens, orange, red, white, and blue dominated the landscape. People danced arm in arm in the streets, singing at the top of their lungs; we all went mad. The Allied forces that liberated us rode through the streets in their tanks, blocked in their progress by the crowds that surged around them. These healthy men looked like the very angels of heaven, and so we treated them. We were free! Others had accomplished this for us; the Dutch could not do it for themselves. These godlike foreigners had come to save us. So it seemed to the child, who knew nothing of strategies and world wars, who knew only that a cloud had lifted, never to come back again. People had acted on behalf of those who could not act for themselves. It happened; it happens.

Things could have gone otherwise for the Frank baby in our village. The Franks, being Jews, were the most vulnerable members of a vulnerable population. The Dutch, though oppressed themselves, were the only ones who could protect the most vulnerable among them. At such times, alliances must be formed among the groups that are deprived of power, alliances that are crucial for the survival of the ones who are the most victimized. Where this type of alliance was not made, or where it broke down, disaster happened almost instantly. In the case of the Franks, the alliance was too fragile. There are opposite examples.

Years after the war, during a conference in New York City, I found myself in a taxi with a group of friends. Because of the size of our group, I ended up sitting next to the driver, and since we had a ride of some duration, I struck up a conversation with him. From his identification tag on the dashboard, I surmised that his name was Dutch, so I asked him about it. "Yes," he said, "I am Dutch, and I am Jewish. I emigrated shortly after the war."

Immediately I thought, How did you survive? He must have sensed my question.

"I was a youngster during the war, and people hid me in the village of Z. There were a lot of us there. Everybody knew the Jewish children, but we all survived because no one would tell the Germans who we were. They were suspicious, of course. They even took one of the leaders of the Underground who helped to hide children and provide them with papers. They tortured him. He would not tell. They continued to torture him, and he still would not tell. They finally killed him. Of this man I have a photograph in my house that will go to my children after I die. The picture has a place of honor in my house, and I have made my children swear to honor it after I am gone."

There were a lot of us there. I sat awestruck. The village he had mentioned was only seven miles or so from the village where I had lived. It was possible, then; it had happened against the odds: The little ones *could* be saved. Though rationally I had known this before, and there are examples available in literature of this type of act, the truth had never struck me like this. The cabdriver's story had emotional force that left a lasting impression on my soul.

Thus my eventual view of women as a deprived and dominated group was forged under the Nazi boot. During the occupation, I learned to identify with those members of a deprived group who suffer most, and learned to recognize the necessity of systemic change. There it was also brought home to me that, to bring about change, there must be people who act in alliance with the powerless. Without being articulated, these convictions were present in their germinal state, dormant for a while but ready to come to fruition in their proper season.

Learning Faith

During the war, church attendance in the Netherlands increased. For many people, the life of faith provided light in the midst of darkness, offered hope in the midst of despair and comfort for pain. This was not true for my family. My father considered himself an unbeliever and had made no formal ties to the faith. My mother, who had been confirmed in the Netherlands Reformed Church as a young adult, was no longer affiliated with the church. We children were all baptized, probably on my mother's wishes, but not without a certain amount of tense argument between my parents and the local church elders. In any case, faith was for me not born as a comfort in dark times.

The first significant event in my life regarding the Christian faith was my parents' sending me to Sunday school when I was six. The emphasis of this enterprise definitely lay on the word "school." It was taught in one room for all the children by my first-grade teacher, who was formidable indeed. All efforts of the Sunday school year culminated at Christmastime. Then a great celebration was held, with children and parents gathered in front of a huge Christmas tree lighted with candles. There we were offered hot chocolate and oranges, exotic delicacies we never saw at other times in those poverty-marked postwar years. The children were expected to have memorized the first twenty-one verses of Luke 2, the story of the birth of Jesus. Over this event the minister presided, a person even more intimidating than the Sunday school teacher. He conducted the quiz on Luke 2, calling on individual children to recite a verse aloud by memory. Year after year, I memorized madly, and year after year I waited to be asked, but it never happened. There I sat, so eager to show my learning, and no one wanted to hear it.

I found being overlooked irksome and frustrating, but the experience put no blight on my spirit. Instead, a pattern was set; thereafter, I connected faith and learning, a connection that was, from the beginning, a positive one for me. I could not go to school until I was six because there were no kindergartens, no places where organized learning of any type took place. I remember the year before I went to school mainly because I was bored. I especially yearned to be able to read.

My mother would not or could not provide me with any help in this direction, or perhaps I did not articulate my desires clearly. In any case, when the time came I was ready, and any demand on my newly learned skills was grist for my mill.

Sunday school involvement had not resulted in church attendance either for myself or for my parents and siblings. When my Sunday school days ended on our moving to another village, the church was still an alien world to me. Also, apart from my knowledge of Luke 2, the Bible was still a closed book. On a quick perusal of the Gospels in our large family Bible, I had concluded that the Bible told the same story over and over again. This seemed to make no sense, but it was not important enough to bother me or lead me to ask my parents about, so I let it rest. The only activity of faith I undertook on my own initiative was prayer. I always said my evening prayers. It provided a satisfactory close to the day, as familiar as other children's bedtime stories. My mentor in this act of piety was my brother, who was older by two years. Since before our move my siblings and I slept in the same room, there was time and opportunity for my instruction and for me to instruct my younger sister in turn. I remember an important theological discussion with her on the question of whether or not it was permissible to pray for candy. I believe we concluded that one could so pray but should not expect candy to appear out of nowhere. It seems to me now, as I look back, that there were bits and pieces of faith, strewn about here and there, ready to be picked up and made into a whole.

That time came nearer when I turned eleven. In the village to which we had moved a new minister drew my mother and me to attend church. In the life of the churchgoing community there was at that time great excitement over a vast restoration project that was about to reach completion. The village church, like many churches in that region, was an outstanding example of Romanesque and Gothic architecture, dating primarily from the fourteenth century. Over the years, the interior had been neglected and inauthentic features had been added; in the early 1950s a project was started to restore the church to its original beauty. At the time my mother and I began to attend the church, worship was taking place in a large community hall; soon the worship services moved back to the church building. There must have been a celebrative event to mark the moment, but of this I remember nothing. Our church was indeed beautiful. The Romanesque nave lent the warm, enclosed feeling that this architecture conveys. On the other hand, the cane chairs installed in place of the old pews provided a sense of space that was enhanced by the tall Gothic windows of the chancel and by the chancel itself, that was empty but for a small communion table. Dominating both chancel and nave was an intricately carved pulpit where every Sunday morning our eyes were turned. The service was simple. Apart from the singing there was almost no congregational participation. The entire service centered on the sermon, which lasted from twenty-five to thirty-five minutes. Regarding their orthodoxy, ministers were judged to be "light" or "heavy" according to the length of their sermons. "Light" carried a slightly negative connotation; "heavy" ministers sometimes stretched the sermon to forty minutes, a length that most people found exaggerated. It was always best to come out somewhere in the middle of these two categories.

No one ever forced me to attend church; there was no lively youth group or other entertainment to attract me. There was only the Scripture. My mother and I kept going, and eventually my father joined us. What exactly happened there in the small, ancient building that could keep a restless youngster interested Sunday after Sunday? There was, to begin with, the beauty of the building and the music of the Genevan Psalter, which even a poor organ and a less–than–perfect organist could not dim. Beauty is a luxury absent in a war-torn world, and our eyes and ears were starved for it. There was the aesthetic pleasure of watching the ceremonial ascent of the pulpit by the minister in his flowing robes, and there was the stark and familiar ritual of the liturgy.

More than anything, however, I learned something there that I could not learn anywhere else, and it had a direct influence on my life. By the time I turned twelve, I had begun to attend a preparatory school in a nearby town that provided me with enough intellectual challenge for the next six years. I read the classics of literature from different cultures, and my school provided learning for mind and heart, spirit and imagination. In church, however, I found a learning that moved me to a commitment. And that made all the difference.

With the fervor of youth, I made my commitment to the

Christian faith, a commitment that was formalized when I was eighteen years old, as was the custom in our Netherlands Reformed Church. My commitment was first of all to God. That this commitment also involved a turn toward humanity did not become a reality for me until later. The shape of my early commitment was one of learning. I became a pupil in the weekly class of religious instruction conducted by our minister. This class had a curriculum organized around the fundamental principles of the Reformed heritage as set forth in the Heidelberg Catechism, a document we studied in detail, guided by the lively and intelligent insights of our minister. I took my first tentative steps on the path of theology in this class. In church I learned most of all about Scripture. A compliment that sometimes comes my way is that I "make the Scripture come alive." It never occurred to me that the Scripture can be anything but alive, for so it was presented to us Sunday after Sunday. The biblical text was unfolded in all its vividness, with all its connections to our lives, directly from father Abraham and mother Sarah, from Jacob and Rachel, and from Jesus and Mary to this twentieth-century community. The text of the Scripture was never just an old story; it always held something new, a surprise to be anticipated during its reading. Above everything else, the Scripture was allowed to have a voice. What I heard was not always easy to appropriate or to accommodate, but I was always caught by it. I learned not to expect to know ahead of time what a text of the Bible has to say. The text was treated with respect; stories were read in their entirety, not presented in snippets—digestible "sound bytes." Sometimes we listened to a whole story cycle, as I remember doing with the Joseph stories over a series of Sundays. The effect of our minister's preaching was to stay with me for a lifetime; I have never forgotten to read the text as if it has something to say, something unexpected, something unheard of if we have "ears to hear." I recognized then what I was exposed to much later in Frederick Buechner's writing:

> At the level of words, what do they say, these prophet-preachers? They say this and they say that. They say things that are relevant, lacerating, profound, beautiful, spine-chilling, and more besides. They put words to both the wonder and the hor-

> ror of the world, and the words can be looked up in the dictionary or the biblical commentary and can be interpreted, passed on, understood, but because these words are poetry, are image and symbol as well as meaning, are sound and rhythm, maybe above all are passion, they set echoes going the way a choir in a great cathedral does, only it is we who become the cathedral and in us that the words echo.[1]

One hears sometimes of the stereotypical Dutch Calvinist being somber and dour. There must be a grain of truth to that stereotype, but I do not recognize it. Dourness and somberness would not have suited me in my adolescence. The exposition of Scripture that I heard every Sunday was intelligent, profound, and often witty. Perhaps because no one demanded that I go to church or believe, faith was never a burden to me. The Christian faith provided me with guidance, order, and a sense of goodness and hope in the public sphere, something that had been missing in my very early years. This faith and its text liberated me from the fear of brutality's logic and presented a universe of hope. The obligations I took on were voluntary. I kept, for example, a strict Sabbath rest on Sunday of my own volition. I took walks, read Scripture, and did not do any homework for my school. I had to work very hard to keep up with my school's curriculum, and the one day of rest was a haven in my week of work. I liked Sundays that way, and these days often wish for their quietness in my hectic life. There were not many taboos on Sunday; the only restriction was that we did not handle money, outside of what we put in the collection plate in church.

In hindsight I can discern points of congruence between the Calvinism of my church and my experience of the war years. As time went on, more and more of the brutality exercised in the extermination camps came to light. One of the most difficult aspects of this brutality was that the perpetrators were ordinary people. These were not monsters, whose faces were somehow marked by the monstrosity of their behavior, people whom any decent human being would avoid. Rather, the torturers in the camps were themselves ostensibly decent human beings who loved their pets and their families, who liked music and literature. Because of the incident in my village involving the Frank family, I was already aware how ordinary, decent people could perpetrate monstrous acts. Though far more brutal, the deeds of camp guards and administrators were on a continuum with the action of the woman who reneged on her promise to keep a baby safe. The Calvinist view of human nature as thoroughly sinful was congruent with my experience.

But the Bible offered hope. All human beings are sinful and, for all, forgiveness is possible. To the conviction of sin and the promise of forgiveness, the biblical text gave a vivid witness. The parade of people that came before us on Sundays from the pages of the Bible were far from ideal models of humanity. They showed, rather, all the human frailty of which we had seen such extreme examples during the war. There was Sarah, who was jealous of Hagar and treated her cruelly; Jacob and Rachel, who cheated and lied; King David, who stole and murdered to whitewash his crime; and Naomi, who expressed great bitterness toward God. These were people like my neighbors and me. These were the people to whom God came in Jesus Christ. In Jesus sin and death are not the last words spoken in creation. Here, too, my experience found a point of connection: Liberation from the war *had* taken place; the last word was freedom.

It was clear how the Jews had suffered more than any group in Europe during World War II. The Holocaust made visible to people the way that Christian anti-Judaic tradition contributed to the persecution and slaughter of the Jews. Of the sixteenth-century Reformers, John Calvin was the most outspoken in a favorable estimation of the place of the Jews within the providence of God. Since Jews held such favor with God, Calvin argued, Christians ought to hold the Jews in high esteem. "For the sake of the promise, the blessing of God still remains among them; as the apostle clearly testifies that it will never entirely depart from them: 'For the gifts and the calling of God are without repentance' (Rom.xi:29)."[2]

There was less room in the Calvinist tradition for anti-Judaism than in other Christian communities, and after the war any anti-Judaic posture became even less tenable. My church experience thus gave a fiat to my feelings concerning the suffering of the Jews during the war. Through my church I began to recognize and denounce the elements in Christianity that had made the persecution of the Jews possible. Moreover, the awareness of this particular oppression provided me with a paradigm for recognizing the oppression of other groups. There is a particular character to Jewish suffering with a particular connection to Christian collaboration in this suffering. Yet, the character of the relation between oppressor and oppressed is similar whenever one group suffers under domination by another. Much later in my life I was able, through my feminism, to recognize characteristics of domination, of which I first learned through my early life experience. One of the most important of these traces was the insight that all domination is ultimately destructive of the life of the dominated group.

Against the dark background of the Second World War, faith had opened a path of learning and hope. When I was eighteen, I took my last course of instruction with our minister to prepare for my confirmation. My father had been attending church with us for some years, and, at the age of fifty-nine, he declared his intention to join the church. Age did not excuse him from showing his commitment by a willingness to learn, and my father and I went to instruction together for six months. Having learning our lessons well, we were both confirmed as members of the Netherlands Reformed Church in the spring of 1959.

Becoming a Feminist

During my teenage and young adult years, I was unaware of the inequalities between women and men. All of the graduating students in my high school class, half of them women, went to university. The fact that more than 75 percent of the theology students and all of my teachers were male did not strike me as odd. No one in my environment encouraged feminist thought. These were the fifties and early sixties, before the women's liberation movement in the United States. I studied, married; all seemed well. Soon after my emigration to the United States, I decided to pursue further study and began doing doctoral work in New York City. While I was going to school, I was immersed in keeping up with my studies and maintaining a family life as a commuter who traveled five hours each day. For years I suffered from chronic fatigue. I was also occupied with family matters and career choices. My pace left little room for alertness to what was going on around me regarding women's liberation. I heard rumors about marches, and people were agitated about Mary Daly, who had just published her first book, but it all seemed remote and farfetched. In hindsight, it seems likely that the separation from my home and native country created the need in me for a long period of stabilization. This separation had initially caused a deep depression, and for a long time I was busy coming to terms internally with the fact of being an emigrant.

Our son was born, I became a candidate for the ordained ministry, and, during the second half of the seventies, my career choice became clear. I was ready to apply for a job. Alas, at that time, jobs in the academic world were extremely scarce, and the prospects of finding something were not good. My husband and I had agreed to make a possible teaching appointment for me a priority in deciding where to move. When there seemed to be no opening for me anywhere, we moved to a new place where he had received a call. We had been there a year when I received my doctorate. Still, there was no sign of work. I had made calls to the different schools in our area, but there were no positions available, especially for qualified persons. Then, in the early spring of 1977, my husband showed me the advertisement for a position in Old Testament at one of the Presbyterian seminaries. For the first time it looked as if there was some movement in the closed job market.

I called the placement office at my seminary. The person who directed this office said she was aware of the opening but had not sent my dossier because she thought the seminary was too far for me to commute. It would indeed have been out of the question for me to commute to a city more than six hundred miles away. I was astounded to find out that it had not occurred to anyone that my family's future plans might be connected to my career choice. My dossier was supposed to be circulating without geographical restrictions. Assumptions had been made about my family and myself without taking into account decisions we might have made or would still be able to make. These assumptions and the control they were exercising over my life could have had devastating consequences.

I had become invisible. The real person that I was had no

effect on the outside world; only the person that I was thought to be or should be according to someone else had any impact. I did not realize this at the time and blamed the director of the placement office, rather than systemic causes, for the problem. Yet an awareness was raised in me, an awareness that my lack of prospects in teaching were not entirely due to an imbalance of supply and demand in academia. It was connected to the fact that I was a woman. I applied for the position in question and was called to begin teaching the Old Testament in the fall of 1977.

How does one become a feminist? My war experience I had undergone without involvement of the will; my faith experience I had embraced with my will positively engaged; to feminism I came hesitantly, with much inner turmoil. It is exceedingly painful to begin to discover the reality of patriarchy in one's life and to begin to name this reality. For me, working outside my home made all the difference. In the workplace, I experienced discrimination, sometimes trivial, sometimes serious. The moment came when I could no longer deny the reality of inequality that was a large part of my life. At such a moment, one has to make a decision. It might still be possible to return to the old way where one is blind but comfortable. The new road seems to provide little comfort; it puts one in a critical position in relation to one's environment, and such critics are rarely welcome. Although the discrimination I experienced was minor compared to that of other women, especially women underprivileged because of race or class, one should not underestimate the constant pressure, the "psychic battering," that goes on in an environment where being male is normative. My own experiences were above all important as they became the channel through which I could identify with other women, especially the most deprived. I made the decision to go on the new road, to face my reality, and, in doing so, to face the reality of all women's lives.

Experiences mark us and open our eyes. In addition, I had become engaged intellectually with the theologies of liberation. Out of a request from a student grew a course in liberation theology that became a permanent addition to my teaching. Thus I opened myself to an ongoing exposure to the theologies from Latin America, black and feminist North America, Africa, and Asia. Liberation theologies are born out of the experience of oppression; for me, feminist thought became firmly anchored in that wider expression of the experience of oppression.

Three features of liberation theology had a direct bearing on my situation. First of all, theologies of this type take a critical stance toward the society as well as toward the church. My decision to face the reality of inequality between men and women had already put me in a critical position to my immediate, ecclesial environment; it also put me in a critical position toward society. Liberation theologies provided me with a solid basis for my critique, since the main representatives of these theologies base themselves firmly on the gospel. The second characteristic, shared by all of them, is an emphasis on the communal and public rather than on the individual and private character of the gospel. My childhood had conditioned me to understand structural injustice as the cause of the worst kind of oppression and to understand individual sin and deeds of injustice within a structural framework. The understanding of sin as social and political, with a concrete expression in societal institutions, seemed a correct articulation of what I had experienced as a child. The third feature is the emphasis on the connection between faith and commitment. It had always been significant to me that to be a Christian meant to have a certain way of life. Yet it was not clear for many years how this commitment would live itself out in terms of human relations beyond the purely individual ones. The question of how the church lives out its commitment to be a loving and just community that worships a just and loving God became most pressing.

The three features typical of all liberation theologies came together for me in feminist theology. Feminist theology bases itself on the gospel and, on this basis, is critical of patriarchy and the context of its theology, the church, as well as its larger context, the society. Patriarchy is a communal phenomenon, a systemic injustice that permeates all of life, as Nazi domination had permeated all of life in the occupied countries during World War II. The connection between faith and commitment took shape for me in a commitment to women. I began to find out that in most instances a commitment to women equals a commitment to the poor. Two basic differences between theologies of liberation and traditional Western theologies are the place where these theologies happen and the people represented in those theologies. In liberation theologies, including feminist theology, voices are raised that have never been heard before. The oppressed of Latin America receive a voice through Latin American liberation theology. Similarly, women's voices heard in the theological enterprise indicate a major shift in focus.

Very early in my career a positive experience began that reinforced what I was learning and experiencing elsewhere. My seminary had on its campus a group of women students who had formed a caucus, as was the custom in many schools in the late sixties and early seventies. This group had lobbied for several issues important to them and to the life of the seminary. One of these issues was the appointment of a woman to the teaching faculty. When I came to the campus, I was aware of the contribution of these students to my arrival. Here again, a lesson learned from the war was brought home to me: Alliances must be formed among those who lack power to change things for themselves so that change can occur. The alliance among women on our campus began productively and has continued to be instrumental in the changes that still have to happen.

Another alliance, formed early in my teaching career, proved invaluable to me: the relationship with the women's organizations of the Presbyterian Church. They provided me with my first major speaking opportunities and with my first chance to write for publication. They encouraged and supported me with their curiosity, their intelligence, their imagination, and their love, and they provided me with a platform I could not have found elsewhere. Within their circle I was not the exception to the male norm, and I could escape from the psychic battering I experienced elsewhere. I found with them a certain kind of safety that may have helped me to maintain my mental stability through the difficult years when I was first beginning to articulate my feminism. Both alliances were essential in establishing a safe place and helping to bring about change. Over the years, it has become increasingly clear to me how crucial such alliances are for women.

In Latin America, the voices of the poor and oppressed are heard through such people as Gustavo Gutiérrez and Paolo Freire. These writers and many others like them speak from the perspective of the oppressed, in solidarity with the ones who are deprived and victimized and who need liberation. As I continued to read and teach liberation theology, it became gradually clear how vast a proportion of today's victims across the world are women and their children. The devastation brought about by patriarchal structures and ideology becomes most visible in the destruction of women's lives. Even had I wanted to, it was not possible to dismiss this fact by ascribing the situation to Third World underdevelopment, because during the last decade it has become more and more evident how high a percentage of the poor in the United States consists of women and children. I had been exceedingly lucky to find a career that would enable me, if it became necessary, to support my family and myself. From what I read the same is true for only a very small segment of well-trained women in professions that until a short time ago belonged to men only. The fact that a few women are present in the workplace to an extent that was once impossible tends to blind us to the fact that these women are the exception to the rule. Indeed, women as a group are reported to be worse off economically today in the United States than they were twenty years ago. Patriarchy creates systemic injustice. Within this system, large groups of women and their dependents are being destroyed by poverty. Unless those who are in a position of relative freedom bond together with their sisters who are in poverty, disaster will overtake us all. When a part of the body suffers, the whole body suffers. A community cannot experience shalom when a part of it is in such pain.

It is one thing to face the inequalities between women and men; it is another to realize that these inequalities are directly linked to the destruction of women's lives. Such knowledge is not easily absorbed into one's thought and convictions. Far more difficult yet is it to raise awareness of this reality in other people, including the victims themselves. Feminism caused me to take a critical stance toward my environment, including the church. The church is also a patriarchal institution, which upholds and supports patriarchy through its language and practice. As I grew older, my early Calvinist convictions underwent revision and modification; feminism was not the first complex of ideas to challenge my faith. There were and are specific points of tension, however, between a Calvinist/Reformed expression of the Christian faith and feminist theology, just as there are specific points of compatibility. These continue to work themselves out through my own particular ways of being and thinking. It is important to recognize that the answers are not in on all the questions. For many women, the authority of the biblical text, for example, is negated by its patriarchal cast. Yet it seems at least *possible* to entertain the notion that the patriarchy of the Bible is not integral to its truth, and feminists *can* maintain a Calvinist stance regarding the authority and interpretation of the Bible. To those issues we now turn.

2

The Reformation and the Bible

The Reformation brought about a major change with respect to the place of the Bible in the life of faith. Crucial to the ideas of the Reformers was the accessibility of the Bible to all believers. Second, they accorded to Scripture central authority as God's word. We will explore here the ramifications of this position and some of the problems it raised in Christian communities that claim a Reformed heritage. The most vital question before us is, How can we appropriate the ideal of a text accessible to and authoritative for Christian believers?

Beautiful Lines

In the restored village church of my youth there was beauty of shape and color. The shape of the church building had remained undamaged through the long centuries of its existence. It was left to the architects of the restoration project to highlight this shape by simplifying some of the furnishings. The most remarkable feature of the restoration was the return of color to the whitewashed interior. When I looked around my church, I saw muted blues and reddish browns decorating pillars and vaults. On either side of the chancel, murals faced the congregation. The colors of these paintings were muted also; the shapes were faded and difficult to make out, as if the artist had begun the work without completing it. These faded murals and paintings were all that could be salvaged of what surely were once brilliantly colored decorations in a church that was built long before the Reformation. One of the direct consequences of the Protestant Reformation was the removal of paintings and statues from sanctuaries, which were then whitewashed to remove all color. The congregation could thus worship in a "purified" or "cleansed" church. In many places, these purification efforts took a violent expression: statues were smashed, paintings were destroyed, and the sacred host was fed to goats. Such violence was certainly a part of the cleansing of the church in the Lowlands, where a storm of iconoclasm raged during the summer of 1566. There the violence was largely due to the political ferment of the time. A populist rebellion against absolute monarchial rule combined with religious fervor in the Dutch provinces to create a mood of destruction. The same motivation, however, governed the removal of objects and decorations in church buildings everywhere. The Reformers considered the church polluted by idolatry, of which the statues and decorations were the visible symbols. Of this pollution the church had to be cleansed.

A standard dictionary definition of "reform" is "to put an end to an evil by enforcing or introducing a better method or course of action or behavior." "Reformation" means accordingly improving what is defective, objectionable, faulty, or not efficient. The Protestant Reformation of the church in the sixteenth century was more than simply a reshaping of institutions and beliefs. One might say that the Reformers aimed at correcting and improving what had become misformed in the church. One of the most serious corruptions, according to Luther and Calvin, was the absence of the Bible from the center of the believers' faith and worship. Calvin meant to place the Bible in a central position of authority.

During the late Middle Ages, the art and the relics as well as the Eucharist of the Roman Catholic Church received the devotion of the faithful. Considered concrete manifestations of the presence of God, these objects were handled by a consecrated class of people only, the priests, who mediated the power of such objects to the believers. Such devotion and manipulation of what was holy Calvin considered to be idolatrous. Visible, material images could not represent the invisible, spiritual presence of God, according to Calvin. Also, there existed no biblical basis for the established devotion of the late medieval Roman Catholic Church, including its hierarchical priestly class. Thus devotion, worship, and clerical hierarchy were grounded in custom. Custom, for Calvin, was that which people create and which soon becomes corrupt, since human judgment is corrupt. Over against custom Calvin put the principle of the central authority of Scripture. Out went the pictures and statues, and the pulpit henceforth dominated the sanctuary. Where once stood the high altar with all its trappings, there stood now, lifted high, the pulpit with its lectern holding the Bible. Where once the priest had performed the mysterious rite of the Eucharist in isolation from the congregated faithful, his back turned to them, there now sounded the clear and beautiful lines of Scripture, in the mother tongue, understandable to all, proclaimed and expounded by the servant of the Word, the minister.

Of course, a great deal of art was lost to the church and the culture as a result of the more violent expression of church cleansing. It is easy today to disapprove of the sacking of churches, the smashing and the burning, and the feeding of consecrated hosts to goats and dogs. Yet one needs to be aware that the actual removal of what once held great power over the mind and soul of the believer was also accompanied by rejoicing as the yoke of idolatry was smashed. The smashing and the tearing, the stripping and the whitewashing, took place in a spirit of exultation. People relished the newly won beauty of their sanctuaries. A profound and sincere piety surrounded the notion of being a part of a purified church. Poetry and prayers of the time, and for a long time after, witness to the gratitude felt by believers for the opportunity to worship in a "pure" church. Not until hundreds of years later did believers feel they could restore the color and the paintings that still remained under the whitewash in pre-Reformation churches. These were, after all, only a muted, partial reminder of what once had dominated the religious imagination. The little color that was left no longer exercised the power to dominate. Its effect only enhanced the beauty of shape and line already present. The lines of the biblical text had dominated the environment for so long that it was not easy to imagine anything else in their stead.

"From the Very Mouth of God"

For John Calvin, Scripture, through the power of the Holy Spirit, is the living voice of God.[1] There are no human writings that are equal to Scripture, according to Calvin; true knowledge of God is made possible only through Scripture. Everything the believer needs to know about God and the manner of worshiping God can be found in the Bible.

By these assertions Calvin denied, on the one hand, that the church has the power to validate the authority of Scripture. On the other hand, Calvin would not have anyone claim revelation of God outside of Scripture. This second attack was aimed at movements and individuals who declared themselves to be directly inspired by the Holy Spirit. According to Calvin, the Spirit is bound to the Scripture—that is, is bound to work through the Scripture. It is also the Spirit who makes the truth of the Scripture abundantly clear, "as clear evidence of its own truth as white and black things do of their color, or sweet and bitter things do of their taste."[2] The intent of the principle of the Scripture as central and final authority was to undermine the authority of the Roman Catholic Church and its clergy and put in its place an institution founded on a scriptural basis. As a result of this scriptural foundation, the visible, tangible—and therefore limited—objects of worship of the medieval church were replaced with the intangible, transcendent power of God's Word.

So much was Calvinist worship attuned to the dominance of Scripture that congregational singing was only permissible if it was based on the text of the psalter, or, as Calvin put it, the "divine and celestial hymns of the good king David."[3] Calvin, who was at first opposed to music and song as a part of the worship of the Reformed churches, had a change of mind on this subject but would allow only the text of the psalms to be sung. He had music composed for a metrical, rhymed version of the psalms in French. Countries that were directly influenced by the Calvinist Reformation followed suit, providing their own translations set to the music composed under Calvin's direction. Four hundred years later, the Netherlands Reformed Church's hymnbook still includes, besides hundreds of other songs, all of the psalms, set to music composed in sixteenth-century Geneva. There were, in our congregation, people who would sing only from the psalms during worship. If the liturgy required singing songs other than the psalms, these believers would not participate. I remember well the few who would pointedly close their hymnals and sit in silent protest during the singing of words other than those composed by the "good king David."

The Reformers' stance regarding the Bible constituted a radical departure from the belief and practice of the Roman Catholic Church of that time. From decrees and statements made from 1000 to 1500 in medieval Europe, it is clear that access to the Scripture for the laity was considered dangerous. The mysteries and knowledge contained in the Bible were thought to be too high for the ordinary mind, and giving the Scripture to unlearned people was at least once said to be "throwing pearls before swine." To understand the principle of scriptural authority of the Reformation, one needs to keep in mind the state of the Bible in the medieval church. Calvin and other Reformers intended by no means to rule out the importance of reason, experience, and general knowledge in the study of Scripture. In fact, they brought all of these to bear on their own study of the Bible. Nor did the Reformers intend to replace the worship of tangible objects with the worship of another tangible object, a book. Bible worship was not what the Reformers had in mind. It was the dynamic, living Word of God that they intended to put in the center of faith and worship. To this living, dynamic Word the believers were meant to receive access through their access to the Scripture; of this Word the minister was the servant.

Not long ago, during the festivities surrounding the opening of the national offices of the Presbyterian Church (U.S.A.), a young woman approached me in the new bookstore. She took me to a table with a display of Bibles and said in an anxious tone, pointing to one of them, "There are books in this Bible that I don't recognize." She had in front of her a Bible that was open to the Book of Maccabees. I assumed this was a version of the Bible with the Apocrypha and tried to explain to her that different communities use different versions of the Bible. I recommended that she stay with the version used in her faith community and that she talk to her minister about the reasons for the different versions. She was not easily satisfied. Still visibly disturbed, she asked, "But what if I am not doing something that is in one of these books? Or what if I'm doing something that I'm not supposed to do?" I tried to reassure her once more and urged her again to talk to her minister. None of my explanations sufficed. When I was done, she looked at me and said, "Yes, but which is the Bible God wrote?"

While I have forgotten my final reply, the woman's question has remained with me. It may be amusing to many of us, but it is also a question that goes to the heart of things. Above all, it is a post-Reformation question. Before the Reformation, the Bible was read and studied in the official Latin version, Latin being considered the holy language of the Roman Catholic Church. This official version, called the Vulgate, was prepared by Jerome around 400 C.E.; it was based on the collection of the books in the Old Testament in the Greek language, translated from the Hebrew for Greek-speaking Jews in Alexandria, Egypt, between 300 and 100 B.C.E. The great humanist scholar Erasmus and the Reformers Luther and Calvin were children of the Renaissance, when the cry "back to the sources" with respect to the Bible meant that it had to be translated from the original languages, Hebrew for the Old Testament and Greek for the New. For the Old Testament "back to the sources" meant also a return to the collection of biblical texts as it had been approved for Judaism in the first century C.E. Judaism had then rejected a number of books in the Greek collection, partly because the collection had become the Bible of early Christianity. From the time of the Reformation on, the collection of books in the biblical canon for Protestantism has been different from that for Roman Catholicism. The Roman Catholic Church reaffirmed its commitment to the Vulgate at the Council of Trent in 1546, whereas in Protestant churches the Hebrew canon prevailed because of the Reformers' insistence on the authority of the Hebrew texts.

Yet the Hebrew or Greek Bible cannot be said to be "the Bible God wrote" any more than the Latin Bible. The Bible for Calvin, and for Reformers such as Luther and Zwingli, was the channel through which God once addressed and continues to address the community of believers. The Bible "flows from the very mouth of God by human ministry," according to Calvin. To the voice of God, speaking through this human ministry of the biblical text, all believers should have access, hence the need for translations. As the Westminster Confession reads, "Because these original tongues are not known to all the people of God who have right unto, and interest in, the

Scriptures, . . . therefore they are to be translated into the language of every people unto which they come."[4]

The importance of providing the faithful with translated texts of the Bible gave impetus for a period of intense translation activity in all countries where the Reformation took hold. In the Protestant churches, not only those charged with translating the Bible were expected to know the original languages in which the Bible was composed; all ministers were required to study these languages as well. They, after all, were the ones whose task it was to explain and proclaim the Scripture to the believers, and they should base their exposition on familiarity with Hebrew and Greek. The knowledge of Latin remained a requirement, since the Bible in Latin retained great importance as a document for study. Of the two languages that were thus added as a requirement for preparation for ministry, Hebrew was and continues to be the most demanding.

For myself as a young student in high school in the Netherlands, Latin and Greek were a part of the required curriculum. While I was still at school, I began to consider pursuing theological studies after my graduation. Thus, it seemed prudent to include the study of Hebrew in my preparation since Hebrew was the only language that was offered as an elective in our school system; the other languages offered were required. The connection I had made early between faith and learning made the study of Hebrew not only acceptable to me but logical and necessary. An instructor came each week to my school to teach me Hebrew. Since I was the only pupil to take advantage of the elective, I received private instruction in Hebrew for two years. I can still recall the mood of those two hours a week of studying Hebrew grammar. I entered a world where the rules of language as I knew them seemed suspended. There was the reading in the "wrong" direction, from right to left; there were the alien alphabet symbols; and there were the mysteries of a verb system that did not follow any sense of time or formation that I recognized. I can still hear the rumbling voice of my teacher; I can sense the promise of beginning to understand more deeply the world of the biblical text, which I had already learned to love, and feel the foretaste of the more adult life of a student at the university just around the corner. All these elements combined to make me feel transported into another world that enchanted me. I still believe that a great part of the virtue of studying Hebrew for today's seminary students resides in the opportunity such study offers for a deeper acquaintance with the world of the biblical text.

The Bible in the Center

Recently one of the former presidents of our seminary, in his commencement speech to the graduating class, pointed out that a denomination declining in numbers needs to look to what makes it distinctive. In doing so, he maintained, the denomination would gain vitality and strength. If he is right, as he may well be, then the denominations that include themselves in the Reformed stream must examine the position they accord to Scripture. The most distinguishing feature of the churches in the Reformed stream should be that they hold the Bible to be central and finally authoritative. There is deep concern these days in many so-called mainline denominations over a loss of members that many consider to be a threat to the life of these communities. Apparently, the majority of people who leave do so not in order to join another denomination of their choice but to become uninvolved; they leave the church for the world. A common complaint of those who leave is that the church "has nothing to say," that it has no distinct voice. A restoration of the Bible to its central place might go a long way in restoring the distinct voice of these Reformed congregations.

On the other hand, lest we feel that a return to this principle of the Reformation would offer a safe return to the past, a type of retreat, let us remember that the Reformers placed the authority of the Bible over against the authority of the Roman Catholic Church and its clergy. Thus, while serving to regain a distinct voice, the centrality of the Bible and its authority may at the same time create an awareness of the impermanence and derived authority of the church as a human institution. As in the days of the Reformation, the Bible may point to a need for a radical reformation of what has become misformed in the church. The authority of the Bible may prevent the faithful from worshiping an institution, even a Reformed institution. Also, by their emphasis on the Bible, the Reformers did not intend to put a book in the center of belief and practice. Rather, they intended to focus belief and practice on God. In itself, the Bible is a book of some historical interest, but with no more power than any other such book; it becomes alive, and its power is experienced, only as the Holy Spirit makes it alive to believers as God's word. As it did at the time of the Reformation, biblical authority may prevent the faithful from worshiping custom and tradition, even Reformed tradition. The Bible as the word of God provides at the same time support and a critique of particular forms of Christian communities.

If the Bible is the living Word of God, it might be as surprising and unmanageable as God. There are different ways to flee into safety from the idea that the Bible provides believers with God's Word, different ways to tame its power.

"How," asked a conference participant, "do you deal with the fact that women are told to be silent in First Corinthians fourteen?" The setting for the question was a panel's response to questions from the floor during a church conference for women. In responding to this question, I reminded the audience of the eleventh chapter of that same letter where the apostle Paul gives instructions on hair: "Does not nature itself," argues Paul, "teach you that for a man to wear long hair is degrading to him, but if a woman has long hair it is her pride?" (1 Cor. 11:14–15, RSV).

In looking around, I observed that I was one of the few women present who conformed to that injunction. In the same section, 1 Corinthians 11, Paul argues that women should not pray with uncovered heads, a rule that none of the conference participants were following. My intent in this response was to show the difficulties of lifting rules out of the Bible and applying them directly to contemporary life. There are many rules and laws in the Scripture that are so bound to the customs and the culture of the time, what Paul here calls "nature," that they are inapplicable today; the book of Leviticus and the Pauline letters contain obvious examples. Of course, the church's approach to ethical issues should be congruent with the revelation of the biblical text. But this congruence needs to be searched out each time anew. The believing community does not know ahead of time how God's revelation will address the faithful.

Putting the Bible in the center of belief and practice means that one trusts God to provide a word for our time and perplexity. It may also mean that this word is different from what one expects it to be. We remember the anxious questioner who was confused by the existence of different versions of the Bible. Her anxiety arose because she surmised that there might be rules she was not following in these unknown books of the Bible. In addition, she wanted to know which version was the "true" Bible, the "Bible God wrote." One way to manage the Bible is to view it as a book that consists mainly of rules; another way is to believe that every word in it is factually true. The anxiety of the person confronted with different editions of the Bible arose because of her view of the Bible as both a rule book and as inerrant. One version, therefore, had to be wrong, the other right. God could not have written two different versions.

Neither approach is what the Reformers practiced. They believed that the Bible is the self-revelation of God. Contradictions and errors are to be found in the Bible because this book was, from the beginning, the revelation of God in the Word as that word is accommodated to human nature. The Bible was not written in the sense that modern books are written. It was not written by one author. It was not even written by a group of authors. For most of the Bible the word "written" is inappropriate; we might more accurately use the word "composed." The Bible is a composite of many different speakers and writers, secretaries and notetakers. Calvin and other Reformers not only radically changed the place of the Bible in the life and worship of the believers, they also brought about a radical change in the interpretation of the Bible. To translate a text is to begin a process of interpretation. The Roman Catholic Church of the Middle Ages had halted that process by declaring one translation, the Vulgate, to be the only authoritative biblical text. The Reformers started the interpretative process anew first of all by their insistence on translations in the different native languages of the people. Although it may not have been their intent, by this insistence they treated the Bible as one would any human text which is removed from its original audience. In addition, Calvin and the other Reformers recognized the need to interpret and explain the translated text. Calvin, whose best-known written work is the *Institutes of the Christian Religion,* spent most of his time preaching and teaching the Bible. In sermons, lectures, and commentaries, he interpreted the Scripture. By his method, Calvin explored the "simple" or grammatical meaning and researched the context of a passage, the circumstances and place of its composition; he sought to define the intent of the original author and pursued the "deeper" meaning of the text. As we observed earlier, according to Calvin, the Holy Spirit makes the truth of Scripture clear. But such an understanding did not mean that Calvin allowed a simplistic approach to Scripture, sitting back to wait for the work of the Holy Spirit to happen. He applied himself to his work on the biblical text with all the knowledge that the scholarship of his day could afford him.

When a school of thought called historical criticism began to develop in the second half of the nineteenth century, one of its ground rules was that the Bible is, above all, a human book, a book with different types of literature, different backgrounds, and different sources; it is a compiled and edited book. The approach of scholars who practiced this kind of study initially caused great tensions in the Protestant churches. These tensions were, however, not introduced by nineteenth-century critics but by the Reformers, three hundred years earlier; Protestantism was late in waking up to them. The tension caused by understanding the Bible both as God's word and as a human book was obscured for a long time by post-Reformation interpretations that placed the authority of the Scripture in the inerrancy of the biblical text. This inerrantist position had become increasingly rigid in the face of developments in science and philosophy that undermined the factual veracity of the Bible. When these developments were finally applied to biblical studies, it was only after a painful struggle that churches in the Reformed stream relaxed their rigid stance.

Calvin, as has already been pointed out, was little troubled by errors and inconsistencies in the Bible. Errors were a result of the fact, in Calvin's terms, that God had accommodated to human frailty in the process of self-revelation. The image Calvin used was that of the lisp or stammer used when speaking to infants.[5] Calvin derived the category of accommodation from his study of classical Latin rhetoric. Accommodation meant the adaptation of a verbal message to an audience, keeping in mind the particular situation, station in life, character, emotional state, and intellectual gifts of those making up the audience. Interpreters before Calvin used the principle of accommodation to explain difficulties in the Bible; Calvin was the first to expand the concept not only to explain errors and inconsistencies but to explain the relationship between God and human creatures. Calvin used, for example, the principle of accommodation to explain the different ways that God administered grace in Old Testament times compared to New Testament times. According to Calvin, God accommodates to human capacity, a capacity that is beset by limitations and sin. The very fact that God's revelation comes to human creatures in the form of the word is a sign of God's accommodation to human capacity. It does not come as a surprise that the principle of accommodation was lost in the post-Reformation emphasis on the verbal inerrancy of the Bible.[6]

There is another approach to the biblical text that is incongruent with the Reformers' understanding of the Bible. Many of us may be quite familiar with this approach, called Marcionism after its proponent, Marcion. This understanding, which began as a Christian heresy, attempts to split the authority of the New Testament from that of the Old and puts the latter on a secondary level in revelatory value. A serious erosion of the central place and authority of the Bible is thereby begun. Different movements and schools of thought have contributed to the erosion of this authority in the past. Today it is advanced from an unexpected corner. Many worship leaders in different denominations use a lectionary for the biblical texts, from which they read and preach in the liturgy of worship. A lectionary provides selected passages from the Bible for this purpose. The current ecumenical lectionary, in use in many congregations in the Reformed stream, is guided in its selections by the Christian liturgical year, for which it provides readings on a three-year cycle. In principle, the use of a lectionary has its advantages, but the ecumenical lectionary in fact contributes to the tendency to lower the revelatory value of the Hebrew Scripture. New Testament texts dominate the texts chosen, and some seasons do not provide Old Testament readings at all. Second, the Old Testament texts are presented in a disjointed manner. Snippets of the Old Testament are presented in a way to sometimes support the New Testament selections, which generally follow a more coherent pattern. Sometimes the meaning of the Old Testament passages contrasts with that of the New Testament texts; many times a clear connection between the texts is lacking altogether. When preachers are faced with such choices, it should not come as a great surprise that they prefer to preach from the New Testament. Where the church thus progressively loses the Old Testament, it is in danger of losing the entire Bible as the foundation for its existence.

In addition, the dismissal of the Old Testament as an essential part of the Bible can be easily accompanied by a dismissal of the Jewish people. It is not such a long step from dismissing the Book to dismissing the people of the Book. For too long, Christians have assumed that they are the logical replacement for the Jewish people in God's plans and affections. Once of this mindset, we are on a road that has its logical end in the Holocaust. There is a difference between the Testaments that should be honored, but not at the cost of losing the sense of the entire Bible as central and authoritative. The Old Testament is also the Hebrew Bible, the writings produced by and for a different community from the church and still considered the sacred text by the direct successors to that community. On the other hand, the Hebrew Bible is also the Old Testament, the Bible that, together with the writings of the early church, reveals the God of Jesus Christ. In Miskotte's words, the Old Testament reveals to Christians "the content, the meaning, and the intent of that which we call Christ."[7]

On a return trip to the Netherlands a few years ago, I attended a Sunday worship service in the Old Church of Amsterdam. As I walked to this church from my lodgings, taking the better part of an hour, life in all its contrast faced me: the beauty of the old buildings, the repelling aspects of the pornography district, the pathos of the pervasive drug addiction, and the unexpected pleasure of a glorious summer day. Like most churches in such cities, the Old Church is not standing in free space. Houses, shops, cafés, and warehouses crowd around the majestic building, which rises above the tumult of the city like a ship riding on turbulent waters. As I entered the church, I was overwhelmed by the peace of its light-filled space. Through the tall, unadorned windows the clear morning light streamed in. During the service, music and prayers,

Scripture and sermon, conspired to create an unforgettable experience of worship. The congregation included people of all ages and backgrounds. From the concerns voiced during the prayers, their deep interest in and love for the neighborhood and its troubled people became clear. The text for the sermon was 2 Kings 4, the story of Elisha and the woman of Shunem. When I asked the preacher after the service how he came to choose that text, he answered, "Some years ago our worship committee decided that the entire Bible should be preached and that we would begin at the beginning. This is how far we have come."

Here was a congregation, conscious of its ministry and involved in its urban context, with a desire to have the entire Bible available through the church's preaching and worship. It seemed to me they were acting on a principle essential to churches that lay claim to the inheritance of the Reformation. In our culture, in those situations where the current ecumenical lectionary is used, believers have become familiar with only a small part of the Bible. Although the supporting ideas are articulated differently—today no one talks of "throwing pearls before swine"—the situation is in fact not so very different from that which existed in the Middle Ages. A group of "experts" have decided which parts of the Bible are fit for the hearing of the believers. Even in regard to the New Testament, the presentation of texts in the lectionary is far from coherent. The members of our congregations have the right and responsibility to claim the gains made during the Reformation and to have access to the entire Bible in the church's preaching and teaching.

The Authority of the Bible

If the Bible's authority, as the Reformers posed, derives from the fact that this book is the self-disclosure of God, it is a temptation to view this book as a container: To get at God's revelation, all one has to do is to reach in or dig deep enough. But the revelation of God happens through the power of the Holy Spirit. On the human side, there need to be certain conditions to make the climate favorable for God's Word to happen. There is, first, the condition of expectant listening on the part of the believing community or the individual, the kind of listening that assumes there is a word in the text that cannot be heard elsewhere. The second condition is that believers come to the text with something to ask; questions need to be posed, concerns and interests voiced. Without the condition of listening, the agenda of the text will not be heard; it will be drowned out in the concerns and questions of the day, or it will correspond to whatever the community or the individual wants it to say. Without the condition of questioning, the Bible will be static, frozen in time; it has something to say, but not to us, not for today. The word that is there will always sound the same if the contemporary situation does not impinge on the text.

We have something to ask—the text has a word for us. Can we get any closer to that "something" we ask? Naturally, different contexts will create different needs, and thus different communities and individuals will approach the text with their own particular questions. In theory, as many questions can be put to the Bible as there are varieties of individuals and groups. It is possible that underneath these variations lie the same basic questions. James Sanders suggests that these questions concern identity and direction for living. Basically, Sanders maintains, the believing community asks "Who are we?" and "How shall we live?"[8] In response, Sanders says, the canon took shape; in the midst of these questions, the canon comes alive. It is possible that we should add to these questions a question concerning God. Does the community not also ask "Who is God?" or "Where is God?" My personal experience with the Christian faith and the church was, as I have described, marked from early on by a powerful encounter with the biblical text. In trying to define more closely how I felt addressed by the Bible in my church's preaching, I propose that the Bible spoke directly to my condition of distress occasioned by the war years. The condition was, it goes without saying, a shared one, though it was not identical for everyone. I have described how the pain and oppression of the war period left lasting scars on our environment. Above all, the experience left overwhelming and painful questions: How could it have happened? How could anything so devastating occur? Within the oppression experienced by all citizens of my country, there was the devastating oppression experienced by special groups, particularly the Jews. As the inhumanity perpetrated during the war years came more and more to light after the war, the questions became more acute: How could anything so inhuman be human? How could actions like these be met by anything but inhumanity in return? Where was God in all these events?

When I was about eleven years old and in the fifth grade, one of my teachers flew into a rage. I had committed some infraction of the class rules. As I remember it, I continued to talk to one of my classmates against my teacher's instruction to stop. My teacher then became angry, as teachers will at pupils who do not mind. There was nothing so unusual about that. Except that my teacher did not just become angry, he became enraged. Except that my teacher had been a victim of a Japanese concentration camp in Indonesia not many years before. His loss of control caused him to beat me severely. Then he took the opportunity to mock me, in my shocked and disheveled state, in front of another teacher who had stepped in, thus shaming me. All of this could happen at any time, in any place, unfortunately. Except that the explanation for this teacher's behavior given to my parents and me was that he had been a prisoner in a concentration camp not many years before. That explanation had to suffice for me. And in a curious way it did suffice. Something is bound to go wrong with people who have experienced the kind of violence that my teacher had experienced. In another way, however, the explanation served only to make painful questions more acute: Who are we that we can behave this way to one another? How did we get there? How can we get out of this trap of cyclical oppression and violence? Where is God in all of this? The Bible spoke to these questions that were raised and kept alive by the memory of the war years.

The Bible has a word for us. It gives us this word in an authoritative way. How is this word authoritative? Perhaps we can approach this issue by using the analogy of a nonbiblical text. In her book *The Accidental Tourist,* author Anne Tyler presents the character of Macon Leary. Macon, in his distress over the death of his only child, is increasingly unable to function and to relate to people other than his two brothers and his sister. His wife has left him, and he has aroused the interest of a young, somewhat eccentric woman, Muriel. Muriel has finally managed to get Macon's consent to have dinner with her, but at the last moment Macon reneges. He attempts to drop off a message with his regrets at her house, but, by accident, he encounters Muriel herself:

> The latch clicked and the inner door opened several inches. He saw a sliver of Muriel in a dark-colored robe.
>
> She said: "Macon! What are you doing here?" He gave her the letter. She took it and opened it, using both hands. . . . She read it and looked up at him. He saw he had done it all wrong. "Last year," he said, "I lost . . . I experienced a . . . loss, yes I lost my . . . ."[9]

"I lost." Three times Macon repeats the word without finishing his sentence. With consummate skill, Anne Tyler authorizes a feeling many of us share. I have never experienced the loss of a child; my sharpest loss was that of my parents. Yet, the writer articulated my feelings. By her sober depiction of the inadequate human being who stands stuttering at his would-be lover's door, the writer manages to authenticate all feelings of loss. Macon's words also mark the beginning of his road to freedom from the bondage in which his loss holds him. The novel speaks both to a human sense of loss and to a sense of regaining self. It is authoritative in the way that it speaks to people, on a deep level of human existence.

I suggest that the authority of the biblical text works in a way that is analogous to that of the novel. It, too, speaks to people on a deep level of their existence. Yet this is only an analogy. The Bible speaks authoritatively in that *God* addresses us through this text at the deepest level of our questioning. For me and many others in my native country, the deepest level of questioning concerned the experience of systemic oppression perpetrated on human beings by other human beings. It was precisely there, at that level, that God met me in the biblical text. Because this is God's word, the text becomes not only authenticating but redemptive. The biblical text witnesses not only to human relations but to God's involvement with these relations, God's involvement in the abyss of inhumanity that humanity creates. Because of this involvement on God's part, the cycle of violence, the flip-flop of oppressed into oppressor, is not inevitable. God's universe is not closed; it is full of possibilities, even for extremely flawed human beings, those with murder in their hearts, those who have committed murder. It was not strange, then, that when I identified women as victims of systemic oppression later in my life, I looked in the direction of the biblical text for both the authorization of the experience and for the redemptive word that opens possibilities for ways of being other than those provided by systems that lock us into the domination of one sex over the other.

3

Women and the Bible

Calvin understood God's self-revelation in the Bible to be clothed in the garb of human words, a sign of God's accommodation to human capacity. In order to understand the Bible it was necessary to explore and understand this human garb. Together with others, and in the footsteps of Erasmus, Calvin emphasized the importance of the "literal" or "simple" meaning of the text; rather than point to what is easy to understand, these words indicated the meaning of the text on a grammatical level.

Methods and Perspectives

The most popular methods of interpretation during the Middle Ages paid scant attention to the grammatical meaning of the biblical text. Words and phrases were explored only in so far as they were thought to point to the deeper truth that lay behind or underneath them. It was this deeper truth that needed to be explored; the words were thought to be figures for it.

Bernard of Clairvaux, one of the most famous preachers of the twelfth century, composed eight sermons on the first half of the first verse of the Song of Solomon: "O, that he would kiss me with the kiss of his mouth." In these sermons, Bernard set out to explain at length and in great detail how "kiss" and "mouth" are symbols for the Trinity and the relationship between the three persons of the Godhead. When we compare Bernard of Clairvaux's sermon with Calvin's work, the modern quality of the latter is striking. Calvin was interested in the meaning of words, frequently explaining the basic meaning of a Hebrew or Greek word and taking into account the historical background of the text. Bernard of Clairvaux paid no attention to these factors. Not all scholars worked in the same way as Bernard, and there were many who did lift up the literal or grammatical sense of the text, especially those who were familiar with Jewish scholarship. But the Reformers were the first to give the literal or simple sense of the Scripture its special emphasis. They paved the way for the study of the Bible as we know it.

There are also ways in which Calvin's comments do not strike a modern chord. Frequently, in his comments on the first five books of the Bible, for example, one finds references to Moses as the author of these books. Phrases such as "Moses intends," "Moses proceeds," and "Moses shows" abound in the commentaries of Calvin. Today such references sound unfamiliar. Historical-critical study of the Bible began with analysis of its first five books, and one of the first conclusions was that Moses could not have been their author. A ground rule for this school of study was that the Bible is also a human book: that is to say, a book with different types of literature, originating from different periods of history, different sources—in short, the Bible is a compiled and edited book. Even for those of us who have never heard the term "historical criticism," this school of thought has had a profound influence on the way we read the Bible. The life of the church with the Bible was not the same after historical-critical study made its mark. Yet in its wake arose many problems. The great proliferation of academic disciplines and advances made in the study of archaeology and linguistics, for example, added complexity and richness to the field of biblical studies, but they also increased the tendency of historical-critical methods to become lost in detail. As the details became more and more complicated, this tendency turned into a problem. Ultimately it seemed that the meaning of the biblical text, once the only level of interest for biblical interpreters and still the impetus for all biblical study, had become lost.

In reaction to the problems of the historical-critical schools, new methods of studying the Bible have arisen in the past fifty years that have tried to provide solutions to the inherent problems of the historical-critical method. One such method is a new type of literary criticism. The literary quality of the Bible had not received much attention from historical critics or from the biblical interpreters before them. This oversight was ironic, since one level of historical criticism is called "literary criticism." But this term did not indicate what one would ordinarily understand it to mean, and few scholars of the historical-critical school had an appreciation of the Bible as literature. They were in this respect true inheritors of Calvin, who had no admiration for biblical style, judging it "crude" and "unpolished." According to Calvin, the crudeness of the writing showed the very graciousness of God in accommodating to human capacity. It is only in very recent history that the text of the Bible has begun to receive attention as literature, with its own literary rules and conventions. Thus a new type of literary criticism has come on the scene. This study of the Bible looks closely at the literary form of a text, tries to understand what literary rules and conventions govern and support the text, and analyzes the effect of these rules and conventions on its meaning. A great advantage of this type of analysis is that, to an extent and on a simple level, anyone can benefit from it, even without training in the text's original language.

Another reaction to the historical-critical study of the Bible came in the form of a rejection of one of its maxims. According to historical critics, the objective truth of the text can be uncovered by studying it objectively. Today, more than a hundred years have passed since the first major historical-critical study of the Bible appeared. Not the least of the advances made since that time is that few people are still convinced of the possibility of studying a text with total objectivity. Everything we are—our experience and convictions, our age and sex, our social conditioning—plays a role in textual study. Subjectivity is today taken for granted by many biblical scholars. Subjectivity is not the same as relativity. Grammar and lexicon still exercise their controls and set the limits for study on a basic level. Within these limits, however, choices need to be exercised and different possibilities selected. Subjectivity is considered a problem only if it is unarticulated and thus exercises unchecked control. One may call this subjectivity perspective or bias, as long as it is clear that nothing negative is implied by the latter term. The Reformers, too, studied the

Bible with definite perspectives or biases. Some of these were directly related to their view of the church and their desire for change of the structures; others were a part of their cultural conditioning.

Although the period of the Reformation was one of great change and upheaval, in one sense nothing had changed, nor was it about to change soon. From its beginnings, the structures of the church had had men in charge of both its organization and the task of interpreting the faith. In the patriarchal social systems in which the church participated, it could not have been otherwise. Men were in charge of administration and learning, in the church as elsewhere. Movements that arose sporadically in which women gained a role of leadership were suppressed in the church. The Reformers stood in a long line of male interpreters who did not consider the fact that women's voices might contribute to scholarly enterprise. Moreover, in the patriarchal structures that dominated the church, women were judged to be more inclined to carnality than were men, their natures closer to the material than to the spiritual world. As the Reformers lived in a rapidly changing world, so do we. Of all the changes that one could name, there may be none so revolutionary as the fact of women's presence today in places where they were not previously seen or heard.

A Special Angle of Vision

When our son was very small and had just learned to walk, he and I took a walk together every day for a half hour or more along the street where we lived. During that time, my pace would slow to that of the very young child, who was constantly stopping to examine the world around him. He would bend down, pick up a twig or leaf, and look at it carefully. He would pause and stare at the trees, at their branches, and feel their bark. He would see a stone and point, chattering, full of excitement. Of course I could not see the world of our street quite as he did. I could not shrink myself to his size and see everything from his smallness for the first time. But I remember how, slowly and gradually, for me too the street began to contain a whole world, how the leaves, the twigs, and the stones appeared strange and wonderful, until I shared at least a part of my son's experience. I began to see things from his angle of vision and saw familiar things as if I had never seen them before.

A number of years ago, a lecturer gave a presentation at our school on a subject he entitled "Models of Ministry." To stir our interest, he had chosen unorthodox examples to illustrate these models. One of them was Joseph as his virtue is challenged by Potiphar's wife. As I was following the lecture by reading along in the Bible, my eyes strayed to the chapter preceding this story of Joseph. I happened to glance at the line "Then Judah said, 'She is more righteous than I.' " I became intrigued by these words and looked through the entire story of Tamar and her relationship to the household of Judah. It seemed to me, even at a cursory reading, that in Tamar one would have an even less orthodox, and certainly a lesser known, "model of ministry" than one finds in Joseph. Questions came to my mind as I read through a story that I had almost entirely forgotten: Why was Tamar called "righteous?" Are other women thus praised in the Bible? Why are her actions, of the most unorthodox kind, not condemned in the story? What is the story doing here anyway, just when the adventures of Joseph have started?

We will have occasion to return to the story of Tamar in Genesis 38. For now, it may serve as an illustration of a change in one's angle of vision. While I walked with my small son, years before reading about Tamar, I had learned to share, to a small degree, the angle of vision that is a child's. I began to notice what I had not noticed before. To him the street was not obvious and familiar. Everything was worth examining, and he chose ordinary things that were so familiar to adults that they had become invisible. Earlier I described the process of becoming feminist for myself as a painful one, which began with the awareness of my invisibility. Once I gained the angle of vision provided by feminism, it became possible to see what had become invisible parts of the Bible. I had thought I knew the Bible reasonably well. Now it seemed that the Bible had been to me a book of men who had interesting things to do and say in the service of God, who even had some women beside them to set off their characteristics. Until my movement to feminism, women were hidden to me in the Bible. I began to discover texts that I remembered so vaguely I might as well not have remembered them at all. Thus, when I first began to see women in the Bible, it was an exciting adventure. There were people here whom I did not know! And sometimes the ones that were familiar, such as Ruth, I did not know as well as I had thought. New people appeared, and familiar ones appeared in a new light.

It has been my practice for some years to tell audiences that I speak to them as a Christian feminist. Since the word "feminist" creates a strong reaction in listeners, it helps to define the term. Many people connect feminism with anger against established structures as well as hatred of men and opposition to the family. According to *Webster's Third International Dictionary,* feminism is both a theory and a movement. The theory analyzes the present structures of the society in terms of their inequality between the sexes and seeks to formulate theories of political, economic, and social equality. The movement seeks to change the existing structures on behalf of equality of the sexes. Feminism views all structures, including religious institutions, as marked by patriarchy. Patriarchy means literally a social organization where the male is in charge of the family. Under this rule, there exists no equality between women and men. Men are in charge of the social, economical, and political structures, structures that include religious organizations and sexual arrangements. In patriarchy, women legitimately exercise power only in the private sphere.

There are many excellent analyses available of patriarchy and the endangerment of life that it has brought about. Elizabeth Dodson Gray, in her book *Patriarchy as a Conceptual Trap,* describes clearly the devastating consequences of patriarchal structures and arrangements for life on our planet. In summary she states, "What I'm saying is that the human species has, so to speak, been driving down the highway of life with one ear completely blocked. Certainly this is strange behavior. For a two-gender species interested in survival, it seems curiously maladaptive and self-destructive."[1] Gray sees that patriarchy has as its logical consequence the destruction of life. Patriarchy has specifically created structures of injustice that are destructive to the lives of women and children. One might object that this is not rational, that the destruction of women would come down to the destruction of the human race. To which one could reply: exactly. Just as the destruction of the planet would mean the end of the human race. It is not rational or logical for human beings to destroy the environment on which they are dependent, and yet we are busy doing just that. Logic does not enter the destructive drive for control. Unless we take seriously the idea that patriarchy destroys women's lives, we cannot change its pervasive structures of injustice.

Abuse, mutilation, rape, and murder of women are occurring across the world. Sometimes these crimes are sanctioned by the society, as in certain medical practices in the United States; sometimes they are covertly condoned, as in the bride burnings in India[2] and as evidenced by the light sentencing received by men in the United States who commit crimes against their women partners. Statistics show that 1,500 women are murdered every year in the United States by their husbands, sweethearts, and lovers. *Time* magazine, in its July 17, 1989, issue, featured a cover story on deaths by gunshot in the United States in one week. During the week of May 1 through May 7, 1989, 464 people died; Seventy-five of these people were women. Of these, 33 percent were shot by a former or current husband, lover, or boyfriend, compared to 2 percent of men who were killed by women in comparable relationships. On the basis of statistics like these, Ntozake Shange wrote a passionate poem called "With No Immediate Cause":

> Every 3 minutes
> a woman is beaten
> every 5 minutes
> a woman is raped
> every 10 minutes
> a little girl is molested.
>
> "There is some concern that alleged
> battered women might start to murder
> their husbands and lovers
> with no immediate cause."
>
> I spit up
> I vomit
> I'm screaming
> we all have immediate cause

every 3 minutes
every 5 minutes
every 10 minutes
every day.[3]

The most pervasive example of the destruction of women's lives across the world, and also in the United States, is economic distress. In her book *Women and Children Last,* Ruth Sidel opens with the story of the sinking of the Titanic in 1912. She describes the luxury of the ship, its claim to unsinkability, and its lack of lifeboats sufficient for the number of passengers. She also points out that at the sinking of the Titanic, women and children were the first to be saved—the first on the first-class decks, that is. On the lower-level decks, known as the steerage section, matters were different. A high percentage of women there died, 45 percent, as compared to 8 percent of the women in second-class and to the 4 of the 143 women—less than 3 percent—on the first-class deck. Sidel compares the United States to the Titanic as she states, "As on the Titanic, the United States is filled with locked gates, segregated decks, and policies that insure women and children will be first; not the first to be saved, but the first to fall into the abyss of poverty."[4]

Statistics and descriptions of the economic vulnerability of women and children come our way with increasing urgency and alarm. In 1984, cautious estimates of the percentage of women among the poor in the United States were that two out of every three poor adults were women. Of course, racism contributes everywhere to the causes of poverty, but patriarchy is always present and manifests itself at all levels of economic discrimination as an extra burden. When we study the pauperization and marginalization of women and children, we study the harvest of thousands of years of male rule. We witness this harvest in the faces of women who work too hard for too little income, who are underfed and ill-educated, and who cannot safeguard the health and well-being of their children. Where women are poor, their children are poor. In our country, one of the wealthiest countries in the world, one out of every four children under six lives in poverty. One of the major causes of infant mortality in the United States is malnutrition.[5]

Perhaps you saw, as I did a few years ago, a presentation on television called *God Save the Child.* This film showed a mother and her eight-year-old daughter caught in the mill of poverty and homelessness. In the end, the mother, knowing herself trapped, gives her child up with the assistance of her social worker. To make it work, she must literally abandon her daughter, a cause of great anguish for both of them. The mother knows that life with her will be a slow death so she gives her daughter life in the only way she can think of. The story was written and acted with power and integrity. In our newspaper, the program received no notice beyond a brief description under the heading "Today's Movies." There it was announced as the story of a woman's poverty "due to an unfortunate set of circumstances." A powerful indictment of our society was thus hidden from the viewers' eyes, and the force of it was blunted ahead of time by the words "unfortunate circumstances," as if these were somehow outside of human control.

Discrimination as I experienced it in the workplace was minor compared to that of poor women and women other than those of a privileged class and race. Yet one potentially health-threatening experience I share with millions of women.

"Do you think that there may be an increased risk of breast cancer if you prescribe estrogen after the operation?" I asked my gynecologist, who was on his usual hasty way out of the examining room.

"Eh?" he said.

"I have read that there is such a risk with estrogen replacement therapy," I explained.

He stopped in the doorway and peered at me over his glasses. "Well," he said, "you can't believe everything you read in *Reader's Digest*!"

I had been scheduled to have a hysterectomy in one month—in my case, elective surgery to ease serious pain. This operation had been "elected" by my doctor. At the time of this conversation, I had just begun to read material concerning women's health. My question originated directly from reading of *Women and the Crisis in Sex Hormones,* by Barbara Seaman and Gideon Seaman, M.D.[6] The doctor's reply to my question was the final straw. I held felt very uneasy about this operation, and he had continuously pooh-poohed my objections. It was time to choose another doctor.

My new doctor assured me that I would only have an operation if I chose to have one, and she immediately prescribed medication that proved effective in eliminating my problem. The treatment I received from the first doctor is one commonly received by women. Intimidation and insults are one thing and would in themselves be bad enough. It is another thing when they are accompanied by health-threatening treatment. Not too long after my experience, I discovered that hysterectomies are one of the most frequently performed elective operations in the United States and that they are very lucrative for the medical profession. In spite of the fact that physical and mental complications arising from such surgery afflict a high percentage of women, it is an operation that remains popular. Perhaps this fact would not cause much surprise if we were to realize that "at a cost of approximately $1,000 each, hysterectomies account for near 800 million dollars in surgical fees per year."[7]

Regarding patriarchy, the church offers little to distinguish it from the culture. In the church, men have always been in charge and theirs have been the voices heard; in sermon and in scholarship, they have set the tone. Although things are changing, the change is painfully slow and sometimes does not seem to be very thorough. The radical shift in student population at the Protestant seminaries, from all male to half female in the last twenty years, is not yet reflected in the structures of the churches to which these seminaries are tied. As I have worked in my school and observed the changes in our student body, I have also observed the continuing lack of opportunity for women in our denomination. In this church, women's ordination to the professional ministry has been possible more than thirty years. Last year, one of the students who graduated at the top of her class in our seminary also won the award for the student with "the greatest promise for ministry." A year later she still was looking for a job. Books are written, and statistics are compiled, and the news is that women have a harder time finding work than do men in the professional ministry and that, when they succeed, they earn less than men do.[8]

The ramifications of patriarchy once more opened up for me the abyss of inhumanity, as my early experience of the war years had done. This time I looked naturally to the Bible to authorize and redeem the experience. The questions "Who are we?" and "How shall we live?" and "Where is God?" took on new focus and meaning in light of the feminist angle of vision. The subject of the first two questions received focus in women's experience: Who were the women of the Bible? How did they live? How were they a part of God's involvement with the world? What does this tell us about how we should live?

When I began my work on the story of Tamar in Genesis 38, I was surprised by Tamar's invisibility in commentaries and relevant articles. Many aspects of the narrative received scholarly attention: the exact place where Judah settled and its significance for the later tribe Judah, the place of Judah in the line of succession, the place of the story in the cycle of the stories about Joseph, the law of inheritance rights of the firstborn, and the customs regulating prostitution. All these and other subjects were of great interest to many scholars. But in the end of the learned discourse, Tamar had disappeared in the mist of the research, less visible than ever.

Calvin's comments were an exception to this rule. He paid attention to Tamar, but his attention was largely judgmental. He observed that she committed an "atrocious crime" in pretending to be a prostitute, and he declared the judgment pronounced on her by Judah justified. Calvin used the text for a substantial discourse on the sin of adultery. The problem with his comments is that they originate from his patriarchal angle of vision, formed by his cultural and religious biases, rather than from the Bible. In fact, the judgments are not warranted by the text itself. Not only is Tamar's presence clear and defined, the only judgment on her is the reversal of her punishment and the words "She is more righteous than I" put in Judah's mouth. She was remembered with honor in the history of God's people and is mentioned in two other places in the Bible: at the end of the book of Ruth and in the genealogy of Jesus in the first chapter of Matthew.

An Eye Opener

This is the story of Tamar, who grew up in old Canaan, just at the time that Jacob and his family lived around the area of Jerusalem. You have heard of the family. There are quite a few stories about Jacob's sons. There was, for example, Joseph, the little brother; his brothers tried to get rid of him. Just at the time when this Joseph is out of the way, one of the older brothers, Judah, decides to settle down and raise a family:

> It was at that time that Judah came down from his brothers and drew aside to live with an Adullamite by the name of Chirah. There Judah saw the daughter of a Canaanite whose name was Shuah, and he took her and entered her. She conceived and gave birth to a son. She called him Er. She conceived again, bore a son, and called him Onan. Once more she gave birth to a son, and him she called Shelah. She bore him in Keziv. Then Judah took a wife for Er, his firstborn, and her name was Tamar.
>
> Genesis 38:1–6

Father Judah is doing well at his job. His wife, in dutiful response, keeps giving birth. All is well in this family. The children grow and prosper, until the oldest is ready for marriage. Judah arranges for the marriage as is proper for the head of the family. Throughout he acts as befits the man in charge: he sees, he takes, he impregnates.

> But Er, Judah's firstborn, was wicked in the eyes of the Lord and the Lord caused him to die. So Judah said to Onan, "Enter your brother's wife and do a brother-in-law's duty by her, to raise up offspring for your brother." Onan knew that the offspring would not be his, so when he entered his brother's wife, he spilled the seed on the ground in order to avoid giving offspring to his brother. What he did was wicked in the Lord's eyes so he caused him to die also. Then Judah said to Tamar, his daughter-in-law, "Live as a widow in your father's house, until my son Shelah has grown up." For he thought that this one might also die like his brothers. So Tamar went and lived in her father's house.
>
> Genesis 38:7–11

Things no longer go so well in the Judah family. At the end of this introduction, there are two sons dead and an unsuccessful daughter-in-law is sent home. The agent of the death of the sons is God, according to the storyteller. But father Judah does not know of the wickedness of his sons and would rather ascribe the guilt to Tamar. There must be something wrong with her! The men that sleep with her seem to die very quickly. Moreover, she is unproductive. Unlike the wife of

Judah, Tamar does not contribute to the increase of the family. In view of these considerations, she is best sent away. Judah, still firmly in charge, sends her back to her father's house. He thinks thereby to protect his one remaining son. In the meantime, Tamar, who has not said a word, who is passive in this part of the story, is back home. She, in contrast to Batshuah, is a barren wife, a woman that is considered at best jinxed, at worst wicked—an unproductive member of the community.

> As time went by Batshuah, the wife of Judah, died, and when Judah was comforted he went up to the sheepshearing in Timnah, with Chirah his friend, the Adullamite. The report came to Tamar: There is your father-in-law going up to Timnah for the sheepshearing. So she put aside her widow's clothes, covered herself with a veil, wrapping herself in it, and sat at the Enayim gate on the road to Timnah, for she had noticed that Shelah had grown up but she had not been given to him as a wife. Judah noticed her and thought her to be a whore, for she had covered her face. So he drew aside to her on the road and said, "Please, let me lie with you,"—for he did not know that she was his daughter-in-law.—And she said, "What will you give me, if you lie with me?" He said, "I will send you a kid from the flock." So she said, "Then give me a pledge until you send it." He said, "What pledge shall I give you?" And she answered, "Your seal ring with its cord and the staff which is in your hand." So he gave them to her. Then he entered her, and she conceived by him. Then she arose and left, put aside her veil, and put on her widow's clothes.
>
> Genesis 38:12–19

The story seems to continue about Judah and his exploits, until there comes a sudden turn in focus and the scene switches to Tamar. Judah's wife dies, and, when the appropriate time of mourning is past, he is ready to go to celebrate at the sheepshearing. People, perhaps those who were in the habit of keeping her informed, tell Tamar of Judah's intended travels, and she goes into action. The act of wrapping herself in a veil constituted advertising herself as a prostitute. Whether she had thought of such a plan for a long time or whether she thinks of it on the spur of the moment, the text does not say. We are told of her turn from passivity to activity with a sudden string of verbs: put aside, covered, wrapped, and sat. The text provides also the basis for her actions: "she had noticed." What she had noticed is that Judah is not living up to his promise, and she takes the initiative. Because she has not received what is hers by right, she begins to act on her own, autonomously. She sits at the Enayim gate (in Hebrew, literally "the opening of the eyes"). At this place, the opening of the eyes, will begin the "eye opener" that Judah will eventually receive from Tamar.

Judah also "notices." But, unlike Tamar, he does not notice correctly. He is deceived on all counts. He did not know who Tamar was before, thinking her to be the cause of his sons' deaths. He does not know who she is now, thinking her to be a prostitute. He suffers from increasing self-deception. When Tamar asks for a pledge, she demands what amounts to all of Judah's credit cards, as Robert Alter has pointed out.[9] Judah thus thinks he is giving a lot. He does not, however, know that in reality he is giving far more: the offspring that he would have denied Tamar. The episode concludes with one sentence; business is successfully concluded, and Tamar is back home in her place.

Judah needs to get his "cards" back so he sends his friend Chirah to ask around in a discreet way, changing the word "whore" to "prostitute." The people of the place will not allow any such woman to have been in their neighborhood, be she ever so politely described. No, sir! No prostitutes around here! The lines of this little interlude echo with the phrase "could not find her":

> Judah sent the kid by the means of his friend the Adullamite, to take the pledge from the woman's hand, but he could not find her. So he asked the local people, "Where is the prostitute who was on the road at Enayim?" And they said, "There was no prostitute here." Then he returned to Judah and said, "I did not find her. Also, the local people said there had been no prostitute there." Judah said, "Let her keep the things, lest we become ridiculous. As for me, I sent the kid; and as for you, you could not find her."
>
> Genesis 38:20–23

All have done what they could, but Tamar is not to be found. Judah, who is afraid of ridicule, does not know that his eye-opening experience is at hand. When the truth comes out, that this woman Tamar is no good after all, his sentence is quick and devastating. Decisive Judah is back in the saddle, issuing commands to those around:

> After three months the report came to Judah: Tamar, your daughter-in-law, has played the whore and now here she is pregnant through her whoring. Judah said, "Bring her out, she shall be burned." When she was being brought out, she sent the following message to her father-in-law: "By the man to whom these belong I am pregnant." And she said, "Look well, as to whose ring, cord, and staff these are." Judah took a close look and said, "She is more righteous than I because I did not give her to Shelah, my son." And he did not have intimacy with her again.
>
> Genesis 38:24–26

Judah must have decided that it was a good thing he had disassociated himself from his daughter-in-law while there was still time. He decides on an extremely severe punishment. Tamar, once more reduced to passivity, (emphasized here by the Hebrew verb forms), makes one more speech. At the very point when she is emphatically reduced to a passive role, she turns active once more. Her speech, at the brink of death, is timely and wise. It stops Judah dead in his tracks; as he stares at his long-lost possessions, he too finally sees. He "takes a close look" and makes his last declaration: "She is more righteous than I." Tamar has played her cards well; her life is saved, as well as the lives of her two sons. Judah now disappears from the stage to leave Tamar in the center. The last scene of the story is the process of giving birth, with one woman assisting another. The scene provides a stark contrast to the introduction, where giving birth was done by someone else and Tamar was surrounded by death and ill-wishers:

> At the time of her giving birth, it appeared there were twins in her womb. When she was in labor, a hand appeared, and the midwife took it and tied a red cord on his hand, saying, "This one came out first." Then the hand drew back, and there his brother came out. So she said, "With what force you have broken out!" And they called his name Perez. After that, his brother came out, on whose hand was the red cord. And they called him Zarach.
>
> Genesis 38:27–30

It will be Perez, the one who broke out ahead of his brother, officially the second-born, who will carry on the family line. But in the story, the last word is Zarach, which in Hebrew means "rising sun."

From my angle of vision, this story of Tamar and the Judah family both reflects and challenges patriarchy. It reflects patriarchy in that Tamar lives in a man's world. She is moved about by the men in charge, even to the brink of death. The head of the household has by law that power over her, a power clearly reflected in the story. Yet Tamar, by acting autonomously in her own interest, which coincides with the interest of her community, moves to the center of the story. Against all the odds, she becomes active. She is the one who "notices" correctly, the one who sees straight. In the story of Ruth, she is held up as an example (Ruth 4:12). The story is not an example of structural change, but it does provide a challenge. The promises of God are here advanced by a woman who engages in unorthodox actions. On the whole, the men in this story do not come off very well. They are "wicked" or self-deceived. God, who is known to be in favor of male offspring in the Genesis stories, here dispatches two sons to die. Tamar is the one who restores Judah's view of reality. The tone in which the men are discussed—summarily dispatched by God or acting as if they are in charge and all the while making fools of themselves—may even point to a woman-centered bias.

Tamar has thus arisen from the text as a complex person, real and autonomous, whether we approve of her actions or not. Familiar and yet alien, she was not like anyone I had encountered in the Bible before. Tamar did not afford me the only experience of this kind. I learned that it is worthwhile to strip away the stereotypical wrapping from the women who walk through the biblical story to see them in the light in which they are presented in the text. Thus the accounts of many women in the Bible serve to authenticate the experiences of women today.

Good News, Women?

To unwrap women from the veils of age-long prejudice and stereotype takes an act of courage. The organization Presbyterian Women participated in such a radical effort a few years ago when it devoted its annual Bible study to women in the Bible. This study was entitled "Good News Women," a title implying both that there is good news about women in the Bible and that there are women who bring good news, the good news of the gospel. All we have said so far about the Bible and women might indeed be considered to be good news. Women appear in unexpected numbers. They are main movers of the plot, they take part in the story of God's redemption, and their characters come out as real and alive as their male counterparts.

But there is more to be said. The Bible was composed in a patriarchal culture and bears everywhere the stamp of the patriarchal structures and the ideologies that accompany and support these structures. In large sections of text, women are absent or are present only in negative images, as in the legal material and in the prophetic texts. In other places, the role of women is presented in a diminished way, as in the case of Miriam and the followers of Jesus who witnessed the empty tomb. In view of the overwhelming patriarchal cast of the Bible, we must ask whether it is possible for feminists to maintain a belief in the centrality of Scripture and its authority. The question of the authority of the Bible is one that preoccupies many feminists seeking to reconcile their Christian heritage with their special angle of vision.

If not all the news in the Bible is good news for women, we need to ask, Is it good news, women? when we look at a text. We need to learn to differentiate between the bad news and the good news, between what is conducive to newness of life and what is damaging to it. The admission that the Bible suffers from a patriarchal cast is a good beginning. Second, not only is the text patriarchal, the religion of ancient Israel and the faiths that sprung from it, Judaism and Christianity, are patriarchal as well. While we intend by this statement to make no excuse for the patriarchal character of these religions, we recognize also that all major religions participate in patriarchy. Neither Judaism, nor Christianity, nor the religion that gave them birth are unique in this aspect. Nor, as it is sometimes claimed by implication, is the religion of ancient Israel at the root of all patriarchy. Such a claim would be absurd in the face of the pervasiveness of patriarchy and its structures across the world and throughout history. Yet, Christians are called to deal with patriarchy as it affects their faith in what

Rosemary Ruether has called their "corner of sin." Third, when we are dealing with the Bible, it is helpful to distinguish between different periods and manifestations of patriarchy as the text reflects them. Ancient Israel evolved from a seminomadic culture to an agricultural one to an urban society. These changes brought with them changes in the status of women. Early hunting-gathering and agricultural societies knew a greater complementarity of work roles for men and women than did later urban societies, as Ruether and others have analyzed the development of male domination.[10] Ruether argues that the transition from tribal or village life to urban life is a crucial one in the development of male domination. As societies enter urban life, an elite group of males accrues political power and knowledge. Women are excluded from these groups. The last major transition in history is to mass industrialization, which caused major marginalization of women in the productive sector for the first time and made them entirely dependent economically. Naturally, one does not find this last stage reflected in the Bible, though it is very much reflected in contemporary western industrialized society. It may thus be that what we have before us in a given biblical text represents an early stage of patriarchy and one in which more possibilities were open for women; although, again, as Ruether argues, we should probably not idealize these early periods in the development of patriarchy and consider them a kind of "golden age" of women's autonomy and power. Ruether points out clearly that these early stages were the basis "for an increasingly repressed role and image of women." "Women's place," writes Ruether, "became a shrinking cage where she was progressively trapped."[11] While I agree with Ruether, it must be said also that the possibility of complementary work roles in the non-urban society created greater flexibility for women's roles, a flexibility one finds reflected in the biblical text. As long as Israel was in its pre-urban stage, leadership roles were possible for women, the memory of which is preserved in the texts concerning Miriam and Deborah, for example.

"In ancient Israel," writes Elizabeth Dodson Gray, "children, along with wives, concubines, slaves, and animals, were all the property of the male, to do with whatever he chose."[12] This statement is true to an extent, although the actions of the male were prescribed by the law and he could not quite go so far as to do "whatever he chose." It *is* true, as Phyllis Byrd has pointed out, that women in the time that the Bible was composed were, legally, dependents. The laws in the Bible were addressed to males and concerned male behavior. As Byrd puts it, "The laws, by and large, do not address her, most do not even acknowledge her existence."[13] In narrative material women are often present, sometimes in a secondary role, sometimes in a primary role; Tamar, Ruth, and Esther are important examples. Sometimes, a central role of a woman has left its traces but to a great extent she has disappeared from the text as a prime mover of events; such may be the case with Miriam.

The most difficult texts to interpret are those in which women undergo suffering, even death, at the hands of men, without a word of condemnation of these actions in the text. Phyllis Trible has called these "texts of terror."[14] To find the "countervoice" to such texts, one may need to look elsewhere in the Bible. In the end, it may be that such texts do not have a word for our time. Other times and concerns may give them a new voice. Reformers such as Martin Luther felt comfortable acknowledging that they did not value certain texts. Luther felt this way about the Book of Esther, for example. The feminist angle of vision has given Esther a new voice.

All in all, the male-centeredness of the Bible should not come as a surprise. While we do not seek to excuse such a perspective, it may be helpful to come to terms with it in other ways. Calvin thought of human capacity as beset by limitations and sin. In God's revelation in the Bible, God accommodates to human capacity. God speaks with a lisp, as it were, or a stammer. Calvin applied this principle of accommodation to explain factual errors and inconsistencies in the Bible. By extension, can we not apply the principle of accommodation to diminish the importance of the patriarchal cast of the Bible? Patriarchy and its companion, male-centeredness, are part and parcel of the limitations and sinfulness of humanity. I suggest that we consider the patriarchal cast of the Bible as a part of the "lisp of God."

The authority of the Bible becomes operative where the Word authorizes women's experience and, at the same time, speaks a word of redemption. For a long time, patriarchy found a support in the stories surrounding the creation, as those stories are told in Genesis 2–3. These stories once seemed to declare explicitly the God-sanctioned nature of male domination and female subordination. Careful studies of these texts over the past fifteen years have revealed a different possibility. Phyllis Byrd and Phyllis Trible, both Old Testament scholars, contend that the creation of male and female was intended for mutuality and partnership. After *both* human creatures disobey God, they face the situation of what life has become as it is described to them by God; that is to say, the words from Genesis 3 are *de*scriptive rather than *pre*scriptive, consequence rather than punishment. The biblical view presented in Genesis 3 is "marked by a profound sense of the wrongness of this order."[15] What was intended in the creation was a mutuality and partnership between women and men. Genesis 3 points to the wrongness of patriarchal domination and denounces it in principle with the line "your desire shall be for your husband, / and he shall rule over you" (Gen. 3:16, RSV). The complementing contrast to this text is Galatians 3:28: "There is neither Jew nor Greek, there is neither slave nor free, there is neither male nor female; for you are all one in Christ Jesus" (RSV). Here the new creation is announced as a fulfillment of what the creation was intended to be.

Another source of a countervoice are the many texts where women are lifted up for special concern, most particularly women who are widows. Without male protection, women became among the most disadvantaged and marginalized of all groups in ancient Israel. They are joined by children referred to as "orphans" (in Hebrew, literally "fatherless", for a child without a father was considered an orphan). The prevalence of women mentioned among the most deprived groups would not be good news and might only serve to verify the experience of women today.

Yet the word is not only one of verification but also of redemption. The texts concerning widows fall into three categories. There are the laws that specifically call for protection of the widow, who is often listed together with the orphan and the stranger. Texts such as Deuteronomy 24:17–22 and many others witness to the demand that was put on the Israelite to provide for disenfranchised groups of people; the widow is frequently among those groups. A second category of texts consists of prophetic indictments against the people for not providing the proper protection, or justice, for the widow. We may consider Jeremiah 7:5–7 typical: "If you truly amend your ways and doings, if you truly execute justice with one another, if you do not oppress the stranger, the orphan or the widow, or shed innocent blood in this place . . . , then I will let you dwell in this place." The third category articulates God's special interest in and advocacy of the widow. For example, in Exodus 22:22–23 we read, "You shall not afflict any widow or orphan. If you do afflict them and they cry out to me, I will surely hear their cry." In Psalm 68:5, God is stated to be a parent to the ones who have no parent, a provider for them, and the protector of the widows. According to Psalm 146:7–9, God watches over such as these and upholds their rights. In their attention to the plight of the widow, the people are to be imitators of God; they will "execute justice" as God does, which in the Bible means precisely to listen to the cry of the poor and the disadvantaged, to join in their cry, to help the helpless, and to plead the cause of those who have no one to plead for them. Systemic oppression of groups is denounced in the Bible by these constant reminders of the need to address the cause of particular groups, specifically women. If domination of women was and is a systemic evil, a belief in the central place and authority of the Bible is inconsistent with systemic oppression of women.

Christian feminism takes as its point of departure the belief that God desires partnership for men and women rather than a relation of domination and subordination. For Christian feminism, patriarchy is a sign of the brokenness of the world, a sign of sin which must be overcome. Christian feminism is also spurred on by hope, hope that things can be different than they are, that they can be changed (and in Christ have already changed) to reflect more closely God's hope for the world. To the question, How can one be a Christian and also a feminist? the reply should be, How can one be a Christian and not be a feminist? Who will listen to the cries of women across the world and in the church? Who will listen and join in their cries? How can we hope to reflect the reality of being God's people if we do not take the opportunity to be heralds of the new creation, a creation unbound by patriarchy? The more urgent question may be, How can one be feminist and also remain Christian? How can one stay in the church, an institution that has supported and advocated patriarchal ideology and structures throughout its history and that shows so few signs of changing? Is this institution capable of supporting a new community of women and men?

Yet the church is more than an institution. It is also the community of faith where a new vision is born. When the spies of the tribes go out and return to tell of what they have seen of the promised land, they report, "The country we explored will swallow up any who go to live in it. All the people we saw there are men of gigantic size. When we set eyes on the giants we felt no bigger than grasshoppers and that is how we looked to them" (Num. 13:32–33). When we explore the new territory of the community of women and men, it may seem that gigantic obstacles stand in the way. But now as then one must proceed on faith in the God of Israel, the God of presence; now as then, there are other voices to be heard, voices that say, "You have nothing to fear . . . the land is a very good land indeed" (Num. 14:7).

4

Explorations in the Text

If Christian feminism is spurred on by the hope that things can be different, how does the biblical text specifically support this hope? The following explorations of three biblical stories may give us some indications of the possibilities. These explorations take their particular character from our context of being both Reformed and feminist.

Being Reformed, we approach the text in trust that it has something to say to us. We utilize all the skills we can muster in respect to our study of the language and literature of the Bible. We focus especially on the Old Testament, in the interest of restoring the entire Bible as the authoritative resource for our Christian communities.

Being feminist, we have something to ask of the biblical text. We mistrust the patriarchal assumptions of the text and its interpreters. We look for the presence of women in the text, and we study the effect of this presence on the events. We listen to the voices of women in the text, their words, their cries, and their silence. We look at the actions of women and their participation in the events. We study why they act and how, and we pay attention to comments in the text on their actions.

Being Reformed and feminist, we believe that the patriarchal cast of the text is not its final word. We believe that the text which is everywhere marked by patriarchy also has the word to redeem and change the structures of patriarchy. We believe that the text has a word that may point us to a radical transformation even of Reformed structures.

Each story presented here must be seen against the backdrop of a different time in Israel's history, and a different social context. The first, the story of Jael, takes place in the framework of the fragile life of a nation whose existence has just begun. The tradition of Jael, preserved as it is in one of the oldest texts of the Bible, Judges 5, most likely represents an authentic memory of events as Israel experienced them around the eleventh century B.C.E. The social context of the story is more rural than urban with an overall cast of the violence of war. God's involvement with the people is described as an experience of a powerful drive toward the survival of the people.

A Blow for Freedom: Judges 4:17–22

The story of Jael the Kenite is a subsection of the longer story of Deborah and Barak. The events described here are part of a pattern in the Book of Judges: Israel suffers oppression from an enemy, Israel cries to God for deliverance, and God sends a "judge" to liberate the people. These judges were military and sometimes administrative leaders who were "seized" by the Spirit of God to execute their office. Deborah fulfilled her administrative duties personally but left the conduct of a military campaign to a man named Barak (Judges 4:6–10). We are probably familiar with the story of Deborah, and we know of Jael and her tent peg. Yet Jael is not often the subject of approval.

The tribes of Israel have been suffering under the oppression of King Jabin and his general, Sisera. Deborah has encouraged Barak to gather troops to fight Sisera at the appointed place. Barak agrees; the battle is fought and won by the Israelites. We enter the story at the moment that General Sisera is on the run, pursued by General Barak:

> Sisera fled on foot
> to the tent of Jael,
> wife of Heber the Kenite;
> for there was peace
> between Jabin, the king of Hazor,
> and the house of Heber the Kenite.
>
> Then came out Jael
> to meet Sisera.

She said to him,
"Turn now, my lord,
turn now to me;
have no fear!"
He turned to her,
to her tent;
and she *closed it with a curtain.*

He said to her,
"Please, some water to drink,
for I am thirsty."
She opened a milk jug,
gave him to drink,
and *closed it.*
He said to her,
"Stand at the tent opening;
if a man comes
and asks you and says,
'Is there a man here?'
Say, 'No!' "

Then took Jael,
wife of Heber,
the tent peg and picked up
the hammer in her hand.
She came to him quietly,
she drove the peg in his head,
so it hit the ground;
he, *stunned, passed out and died.*

Then, look, Barak, in pursuit of Sisera.
Then came out Jael to meet him.
She said to him,
"Come, and I'll show you
the man you are after."
So he came to her,
to her tent;
and, look, Sisera
fallen, dead,
the peg in his head.

Judges 4:17–22

Even though Deborah broke through the boundaries of what traditionally belongs to a woman's role in patriarchal structures (by taking on the public role of political leadership), she did not entirely break with the psychological ideal of what is acceptable behavior for a woman; she let a man do the actual fighting. It is possible to approve of her. It is much harder to approve of Jael and to view her actions as redemptive. Commentators are quick to judge Jael's deed in very negative terms; she is called deceitful, a coward, and an assassin. Many interpreters eloquently denounce Jael's lack of hospitality, especially the sacred hospitality of the desert.

The story of Jael and Sisera concerns refuge. Sisera needs refuge, and he takes it in the wrong place. His error of judgment costs him dearly, for the wrong person, or the unexpected person, takes up peg and hammer to kill. It does not fit his ideas of femininity any more than it does ours. But whatever may be said of the patriarchal cast of the biblical text, it is not hampered by such assumptions at this point. Two women are involved in waging war. War is, after all, upon them, and they seek a solution to end the violence. The primary violence of the story does not come from Deborah, Barak, or Jael but from King Jabin and his general, Sisera.

In my translation, I have attempted to keep the rhythms and repetitions of the Hebrew text. My translation is therefore quite different from most available translations. There are also some places where the Hebrew is obscure, and I have chosen to treat these passages differently from other translators. (The most radical differences are italicized.) Because of this obscurity, the correctness of any translation is debatable. The interesting fact here is that translators have so uniformly put Jael in the most negative light possible. All have Jael covering Sisera with something and killing him while he is asleep. The peg, in a particularly gruesome detail, is supposed to have gone through his head, then into the ground, thus pinning Sisera down, as it were. Many commentators wag an admonishing finger at Jael for this accumulation of deceptions.

What do we see when we look at this episode? Here comes Sisera, panting, pursued by his victorious enemy, Barak, to the place of one who is supposed to be on his side. The text states that he ran to the tent of Jael, the "wife of Heber the Kenite." We note how Jael is identified by her relation to her husband. This sets up the assumption that her husband's alliances are her alliances, too. Who would doubt it for a moment? Not Sisera. He knows that there is peace between his boss and the man to whom this woman belongs, and from his point of view it is logical for her to give him shelter. He does not know that Jael is about to break the rules in a major way. When she says "This way, my lord," he does not have to think twice.

Once inside, he asks her politely enough for something to drink. As soon as she has given him what she has, milk, his politeness is a thing of the past. He commands her as he would any of his soldiers: "Stand . . . say." Do this, do that! Jael, the wife of Heber, picks up the tools to which her hands are accustomed, the peg and hammer for setting up the tent—which was women's business—and coming up to him softly she kills him—which was not women's business. She kills him, but not while he lies asleep. The word order would make no sense in the Hebrew, and the word "fallen," used in the last lines, is always used of what once was upright. He is probably sitting down, perhaps crouched, perhaps with his head on his knees, and she probably hits him in the neck. One sure blow, and Sisera of the mighty chariots and cruel oppression is history. When Barak finally catches up, it is to see the victory snatched from his hand, as his mentor Deborah had foretold.

What kind of man did Jael see coming toward her tent? When he is introduced in Judges 4, Sisera is named as one who had "nine hundred chariots and who oppressed the people cruelly for twenty years" (Judg. 4:3). That may sound somewhat stereotypical and unspecific, but we get a better idea of Sisera's brand of oppression from Judges 5:28–30. There Sisera's family is described as anxiously awaiting his arrival. His mother and her attendants ponder what could be delaying Sisera from his victorious return, and they soon come up with the answer: "Are they not looting, dividing the spoil? / One or two girls for every man!" (Judg. 5:30). Rape has always been a part of war and an excusable delay for any warrior. Oh, Jael has seen Sisera! She has seen the mighty hero come down her mountainside and practice his brand of oppression. She has seen him, she knows him, and she is committed to getting rid of him. His presence, even in defeat, is a danger and a threat to her well-being and the well-being of every woman.

So Jael does what not many of us would have the courage to

do. She invites a known rapist into her tent, and then, without hesitation, using what she has and what she knows, with skill and determination, she kills him. Not a "nice" story, but then the times were not nice, and Sisera was not a nice man. Talking about desert hospitality in the face of this reality is inappropriate.

I remember my friend Susan from my university days in the Netherlands. She had been just twenty years old when World War II broke out. She was a gentle person who had been gently brought up in a pacifist family. Soon after the beginning of the war, she and her parents became involved in protecting Jewish lives. Susan became a member of the Dutch Underground. One day as she opened the back door to her family's house, an officer of the German SS came in through the front. In this typical Dutch house, one corridor ran the length of the house with the rooms off to each side. As she told me the story, twenty years later, her voice shook. "What was I to do?" she asked. "There were Jewish children in the house. I pulled out my gun and killed him." Like the killing of the SS officer, Jael's deed of violence has to be seen within the context of her violent surroundings. What makes her actions meaningful is not the quality of violence but the fact that she acts on her own alliances with those who are oppressed. Jael does not act as "the wife of," as Mrs. Heber Kenite, even though she is introduced that way. She does not act in a manner that is prescribed for her; she acts out of devotion to the oppressed and the God of the oppressed. The storytellers of Israel and the poets who were among those delivered from oppression painted Jael in a positive light. They praised her extravagantly, in fact, calling her "most blessed of women," a term of praise reserved elsewhere in the Bible only for Mary, the mother of Jesus, and for Judith in the Apocrypha:

"Most blessed of women," the poets sang:

> Most blessed of women, Jael,
> —wife of Heber the Kenite—,
> of tent-dwelling women most blessed!
> Water he asked, milk she gave;
> in a precious bowl she brought him cream.
> Her hand to the peg she stretched,
> her right hand to the worker's hammer.

She hammered Sisera, she crushed his head,
she battered and pierced his head.
Between her feet, he sank, he fell, lay still;
between her feet, he sank, he fell,
where he sank, he fell, dead.
Judges 5:24–27

Rather than at a man, Jael struck at the root of the assumptions of patriarchy. She struck a blow for freedom, because she refused to act on the expectations set up for her by a patriarchal society; she deceived only those who were self-deceived. Sisera is self-deceived enough to come into her tent and to think he has something to fear from a man coming by. He instructs Jael to reply in the negative if a man comes to ask, "Is there a man here?" When the man, Barak, arrives and looks into Jael's tent, there is no longer a man there! Because of Jael's courage and determination, her devotion to Israel and to the God of Israel, the people were saved for another period of time from their oppressors. Rather than at a man, Jael struck also at the violent embodiment of patriarchy, the "masculinity run amuck"[1] that lies at the heart of patriarchy. There he lies, Sisera, undone by his own stereotypes. The enemy of the realm of God, the one who knew no devotion except to violence—there he lies, the spoiler of women, spoiled by the hand of a woman.

The most remarkable feature of the story in Judges 4 may be the way in which the text plays with the assumptions and stereotypes of patriarchy to turn them upside down. First, in a patriarchal world, a woman's identity is defined by her relationships to the men in her life. Second, the proper sphere of activity for a woman is the family and the home rather than the public arena, according to patriarchal arrangements. Third is a psychological expectation that a woman's role is marked by a "service" posture. Jael is expected to welcome and to nurture even the enemy who seeks refuge in her tent. Finally, women are supposed to follow rather than to lead, to respond rather than to take the initiative. The commentators who upbraid Jael for her lack of hospitality and her use of violence are reacting out of deep-seated prejudices about the posture of women in the world rather than out of an understanding of desert hospitality.

Sisera epitomizes patriarchy not only in his violence but also in his view of Jael. He sees coming toward him Jael, "wife of Heber." Knowing who Heber is, he thinks to know his wife. Her invitation confirms his expectations, as does her gift of shelter and nourishment. She responds positively to him by standing guard for him. Even the peg and hammer in her hand only indicate "women's work." Thus the storytellers have lulled the audience adroitly to sleep, only to bring it to a rude awakening by the revelation of Jael's true intentions. It is a shock to the system and to all systems founded on and supported by patriarchal assumptions.

The patriarchal assumptions that operated in Jael's time are still firmly in place today, and the violence that dominated women's lives then is present now. The story authenticates women's experience. Because it unmasks the stereotypes as wrong and dangerous for those who act upon them and because the reversal of stereotypes engenders liberation, the story at the same time opens the way for a redemption from patriarchy. The one who dies here is the cruel oppressor, who epitomized patriarchy, who advocated violence, and who perpetrated violence, especially toward women. Insofar as Sisera embodies patriarchy and its consequences, we can view his death positively. The one who lives is Jael, who by her deed of courage freed herself, her people, and, most of all, the women of this people from the violence of the warrior rapist.

Recalling the questions we ask of Scripture regarding our identity and our actions, we can view the story of Jael as lifting the veil that has been cast over women's identity. We know at least who we are not: We are no longer defined by roles and expectations that are destructive to women's lives. As for us, we need to step out of the cover of our tent, say farewell to the safety of that position, and come toward that which threatens us to confront it. How we then act will depend on our circumstances, but our actions will depend on a choice *we* have made. The God of Israel often takes a stand on the side of the oppressed. That is also where Jael takes her stand, on God's side, the side where the structures of the powers-that-be are overhauled rather than maintained. Such freedom is not bought easily or without cost; many will wag a finger at us for our "lack of desert hospitality," but without our active mediation nothing will change, or things will change only for the worse. The following stories illustrate this point vividly.

A Woman Cries: 2 Kings 4:1–7

> While there is clearly much truth to the statement that race and class have been major determinants of poverty in this country, women as a group, including middle and sometimes even upper-middle class women, have recently become far more vulnerable to poverty or near-poverty than their male counterparts. . . . It is clear that some of the key causes of poverty among women are fundamentally different from the causes of poverty among men and that the same remedies cannot be implemented exclusively. The lives of the majority of women reflect a different reality.[2]

The story of the woman who cries to Elisha for help is a part of the cycle of stories about the prophet Elisha. While the final edition of the Books of the Kings did not take place until after the sixth century B.C.E., the Elijah and Elisha stories certainly predate that time. These cycles may well have circulated independently, not too long after the events in the ninth century of which they speak. They were collected perhaps by the disciples mentioned in our story. The social and political context is the settled, urban, centrally administered society of northern Israel. The religious context is the prophetic movement, which was growing in importance at that time. From its roots as a phenomenon that included ecstasy and miracle-working, it eventually became the critical and revelatory instrument by which people and rulers in Israel were faced with the will of God. Elijah and Elisha function on both levels as critics of government and society. They reflect both the mystery and power of God's presence as well as God's zeal for a just society. Because of their critical stance toward the country's administration, such prophets and their circle lived on the margins of the society:

> And a certain woman
> *from the women among the prophet's disciples*
> cried to Elisha,
> "Your servant, my husband, is dead.
> And you know that your servant
> was one who feared the Lord.

Now the creditor has come
to take both my sons
for himself as slaves."

Then said to her Elisha,
"What shall I do for you?
Tell me, what have you got in the house?"
She said, "Your servant has nothing
in the house
but a flask of oil."

He said, "Go, ask for yourself
containers from outside,
from all the neighbors:
empty containers, not too few.
Then go in, close the door
on yourself and your sons,
and pour into these containers.
Put aside what is full."

So she went from him.
She closed the door
on herself and her sons;
they brought, she poured.
When the containers were full,
she said to her son,
"Bring me another container."
He said to her,
"There is no other container."
Then the oil stopped.

She came and told
the man of God.
He said, "Go, sell the oil,
repay your debts,
then you and your sons
can live on the rest."

2 Kings 4:1–7

The only significant difference between my translation and more traditional ones occurs in the first verse (the phrase is italicized). I have read the words to mean that here was a woman who herself belonged to the circle of disciples. The

Hebrew can also be understood to say that she was the wife of a disciple, as the Revised Standard Version has it: "the wife of one of the sons of the prophets." The "sons of the prophets" are commonly understood to be disciples who followed them, learned from them, perhaps took down their words, and wrote stories about them. Since female prophets are mentioned four times in the Hebrew Bible, the disciples of Elisha may well have included women (see Ex. 15:20; 2 Kings 22:14—2 Chron. 34:22; Isa. 8:3; Neh. 6:14).

In the records of this period, the time of the kings of Israel and Judah, women are mentioned mostly as being active on the periphery of society, involved somehow with the prophets' circles. In particular, the stories of the prophets Elijah and Elisha contain a number of episodes with women as the central characters. But none of the women who have connections with Elijah and Elisha, as the prophets move about the countryside, receive a name. They may at most be called by the place where they live, as the woman from Shunem is called the Shunemite in the story of 2 Kings 4:8–37. The woman in our story does not receive even that much identity. The text reveals only the facts about her: She is a woman, she is a widow, she is a widow with children. Her name is numerous, and she has many faces. She moves on the periphery of society where she has found her own circle of belonging. But the thread by which she has held on to her security has become more and more worn, up to the moment our story opens. This woman has seen hardship, and she has certainly known grief. Yet she has held her peace. Now something has happened to move her out of her silence, her muteness, and she gives voice to her pain. She cries.

It is necessary that the woman of Elisha's circle voice her pain and name it. Until she does this, her situation will not change. It is not easy to come to this point, to find "the words to say it."[3] In the play *The Miracle Worker*, Annie Sullivan tries to teach Helen Keller, who was born deaf and blind, to connect the name with the object named. Her ceaseless efforts tire even this tireless human being as Sullivan repeats, over and over, almost desperately, "This is the thing. It has a name!" Helen discovers the connection in the final and most dramatic moment of the play. It is indeed a great moment when we find the name to express the thing. One of the first feminists to emphasize the importance of naming was Mary Daly. Women have been robbed of the power to name; it is an essential step for us to find words for our experience.

Without this "cry," nothing will change. Much stands in the way of its being uttered, however. The words to halt us may be "Things are not as bad as they seem" or "They will improve shortly"; we may hear that we have a life that is "still a lot better than that of many." We may hear about other much more "important" problems. We may have internalized these objections, so that they seem like our own hesitations. We may suspect there will be no one to listen to us. Crying is "negative"; one can get so much farther by taking a positive approach, or so we are told.

What does the woman cry to Elisha? She cries her pain and deprivation, of course: "Your servant, my husband, is dead," is her opening line. She could have lived with that pain, but now her children are also to be taken from her, and she knows she is doomed. Yet her cry contains more than her pain. It also implies a protest and a reproach. The Hebrew verb that is used here is above all a cry of protest and distress under oppression. It is the cry that reaches directly to God's ear. "Your servant": the woman begins her complaint pointedly. Was not her husband one who feared God? Was he not one of Elisha's? Had she cried out earlier when the creditor was at the door? Does Elisha not bear some responsibility toward her? What "man of God" is he that he can let those of his most intimate circle starve?

Elisha was the disciple of Elijah. In many ways a powerful man, he was a prophet enmeshed in the politics of his country, the familiar of rulers and kings. He might have been irritated by the cries of the woman. He has, after all, more important things to do. Elisha was, however, most of all a "man of God"; that is to say, one who is in the service of God, who acts on God's behalf toward those who call on him in their need. Elisha has something to teach about the behavior of those who act in God's place, who call themselves "people of God."

First of all, Elisha listens. Listening is difficult; listening to cries of pain and protest is even more difficult. We know it already, and we don't want to hear it again, that long shopping list of troubles. We want to be positive. We don't want to feel guilty again; we have heard the statistics before. Give us something to do, point us to some solutions, or list some other problems, for a change! Elisha listens, and then he has a question. "What shall I do for you?" indicates that he does not assume to know ahead of time what she needs. He does not provide her with a program based on false assumptions of the cause of her pain. He ponders what he, Elisha, can do. Next, of all things, he has the nerve to ask for resources from the resourceless human being in front of him. "What have you got in the house?" What a laugh! What could someone like this have!? Her response, "Your servant has nothing but a flask of oil," expresses only her lack of provision and forces her to name her deprivation once more. Why ask her to state it again? Elisha knows, however, that the change must begin with what she has. "Nothing but a flask of oil" will have to do.

Who was Elisha? A prophet, a man, a powerful man, a dangerous man even, a man who moved within the centers of power, and yet an empty-handed man who lived on the margin with the powerless. A critic of society and of faith, a living indictment against the powers-that-be, was Elisha. A "troubler of Israel," his predecessor Elijah was once called by the king. To such a one the woman comes with her cries. These may be the only ones who can listen to the reality of deprivation and respond to it. The power brokers, the rulers and potentates, and the administration are "inept at listening," as Walter Brueggemann has said.[4] The prophets are the ones who point out that there is no peace and that all so-called peace is false as long as people go hungry and are without shelter.

Today, as in the days of Elisha, help will come for the destitute and deprived when their cries are heard by the representatives of God. When these join in their cries, hope for new life can be found. Out of such an alliance, between those who have the words to cry and those who hear them, a new community of shalom may grow. Across lines of race and class, such alliances may yet change the world.

There have been a number of occasions when I experienced the presence of those who knew how to stand beside me when I was in need; one particularly memorable incident happened when I was on my way to Stony Point, New York. After a long drive from my hometown that began the previous day, I approach New York City at midafternoon from the New Jersey side of the Hudson River. Thankful that it is nowhere near the rush hour, I find the streams of traffic coming out of and going into the city intimidating enough. It seems a long time ago that it was my daily lot to enter and leave this metropolis. I know I will have to make a turn onto the Palisades Parkway just before the George Washington Bridge. In the interests of time, I have chosen the express road instead of the one with local exits, and now no exits appear at all—I seem to be cut off from the possibility of making any turn. The bridge, with its impressive span over the Hudson River, comes closer and closer. At last, I find myself bound to cross the toll bridge, which means losing time and having to find my way back, including finding the correct turn from the other side of the bridge.

Telling myself I have done this in the past and surely there will be someone to tell me how to make my way back from the other side of the river, I grip the steering wheel and drive up to the tollbooth. To my right, cars hum steadily past the booths as I roll down my window to try my luck with the attendant. He happens to be a large man, towering almost out of my sight. He watches me silently and patiently as I stammer out my predicament and request. He nods and restates my problem: "You have made a mistake." "Yes," I say. "Could you tell me how to get back the right way, once I am across?" "Hold on!" says the tollbooth attendant. I wait quietly, thinking that he is figuring a way to phrase his directions to this dim person from elsewhere. Behind me a line of cars gets longer and longer, to my right the steady stream hums on. "Perhaps I can ask when I am on the other side?" I offer timidly. The tall black man in the booth lifts his hand and says once more, "Hold on!" I see that he is speaking into some kind of communications device, and I wonder what he is up to, when he leans out of the booth and points across the tarmac on my right. "Do you see that gate?" he asks. I stare hazily into the distance and nod. He, obviously not trusting my easy assent, insistently asks, "Do you *see* it?" I finally locate it and say so. He nods, satisfied, and says, "You go there, and ask for directions." "But, but—" I stammer. "Hold on!" he commands one more time. And I realize then what he has in mind. The ten tollbooths on my right no longer are letting cars through;

the humming stream has stopped as my helper closed them down, one by one, and I cross the tarmac's wide expanse much as the Israelites once crossed the Red Sea. At the gate, which opens almost miraculously, a kind police officer gives me directions, and I am once more on my way.

That tollbooth attendant will live forever in my memory as one who knew how to listen and respond to need. He went beyond what was humane and nice and did the deed which we expect so little that it takes us awhile to catch on to what is happening. He, a black man, closed down a row of tollbooths, on a busy day, for a white woman. Here was one who listened to the cry and brought about deliverance. Perhaps he knew how it felt to be lost without help. I do not know for sure, but I suspect that he did, for such are the ones who are capable of bringing about miracles.

Before the miracle occurs in 2 Kings 4, the woman has a part to play. She needs to ask for empty containers from the neighbors. This may not seem such a strange activity until we give it some thought. People who have nothing do not usually go around asking for containers into which they can put nothing. They might more logically ask for the stuff to put into the containers. One wonders what the neighbors say when she comes around. She, a "have-not," has to act as if she has enough to fill many containers. She needs help from outside, from her community, and this community's awareness of her predicament needs to be raised before things can happen; to an extent, the size of the miracle depends on her courage to ask for many containers as well as on the generosity of her community. Once she has poured the oil into all the containers, there is enough for the creditor as well as for herself. The miracle provides her with enough capital for a new, independent life, and Elisha trusts her to take care of it. Elisha is the "man in charge," yet he does not act like a patriarch. He does not decide that he knows automatically what is best for the woman. He does not send her away, but neither does he create a new dependence for her once she has been delivered out of her immediate predicament. In the end, her life no longer depends on the creditor, or her husband, or her sons, or even on Elisha, but only on what she herself can do with her newly found resources. She is then on her own, with enough capital to take care of herself and her family and with a guaranteed income, the only way that she can escape the trap of poverty.

A sign of the patriarchal, androcentric bias in the story is that the woman does not receive a name. Very likely, the storyteller intended to emphasize Elisha's importance in performing miracles. Giving the woman a name would only distract from the attention that should properly go to Elisha. Or the woman's name was indeed forgotten, a sign in itself of who is important and who is not according to those who pass on the stories. Whether wife of a disciple or a disciple herself, she comes nameless, deriving importance only from belonging to the circle of Elisha, whose name, "God saves," looms large. What doesn't have a name can easily be ignored or forgotten. The lack of a name here can help to underscore the understanding that what once was nameless must be articulated and defined, must be named, even as the woman named her pain and despair in the story.

Second Kings 4:1–7 is a story that confirms poverty and dependence as a mark of the lives of women and their children in a patriarchal world. I have already indicated this most pervasive sign of the destruction of women's lives. There may be no more succinct way to express this fact than by the following statement from a United Nations report: "Women make up half of the world's population, work almost two-thirds of all man-hours [*sic*], receive a tenth of the world's income, and own less than a hundredth part of the world's wealth."[5] In its concern for the welfare and protection of widows and orphans, the biblical text also reflects the dark side of this reality. The woman of Elisha's circle is dependent on the males around her, a dependence that shows itself most painfully when she loses her most significant support, her husband. Most translations emphasize her dependence by introducing her as the wife of one of the disciples of Elisha. In either case, as the wife of a disciple or as a disciple herself, she turns to Elisha as the next responsible male in her environment. It is, after all, within the circle of Elisha, of those who "fear God," that these circumstances exist. The destructive results of patriarchal structures mark also the circles where one might expect a more pronounced effort toward changing those structures. In the words of the World Council of Churches' *Justice, Peace, and the Integrity of Creation* document, "Biblical faith affirms that both women and men—and the two together—are created as 'image of God.' Yet, we are waiting still for the churches clearly to denounce the sin of sexism, actively to support women in their struggle against oppression, and concretely to provide opportunities for women to bring all their gifts into the life and ministry of the churches."[6]

If the text thus confirms the realities not only of the world of Israel but those of today's world and church as well, it also provides clues for change. Change can begin in the life of a woman when she finds words for her pain. No matter how strong the pressure to stifle those voices that give a name to the suffering of women, we cannot let up on our efforts to describe this suffering, to document it, and to raise our voice in protest. Second, the presence in the text of someone who hears the woman's cry and who teams up with her to relieve her suffering and eliminate her dependence points to the need for partnership between those who cry and those who are willing to hear the cry, even if hearing that cry means being implicated in its charge. How this miracle happens, we do not know. It happens in the secret of the heart, as the oil begins to flow behind closed doors. Miracles in the Bible are always a sign of God's presence. When the disciples of John the Baptist ask Jesus whether he is the one John had been waiting for, Jesus points to the miracles that are happening as signs of the messianic presence (Matt. 11:2–6; Luke 7:18–22). These miracles include the fact that "the poor have good news preached to them." Miracles are signs that God opens up possibilities where hope and possibilities seemed lost.

"A woman cries." There is one who listens to her cry, and things begin to happen. The woman of Elisha's circle moves out of her isolation into her community; neighbors provide containers, children are saved, and a woman gains her independence. The miracle of the oil that filled all the containers is a symbol of hope in the story that we do not live in a closed universe. Rather than pointing to an easy solution, impossible in the "real" world, the miracle of the oil points to the miraculous possibilities embedded in the reality of God's grace. What could be more miraculous than a community among us where patriarchy and its devastation are things of the past, a community of those interested in the shalom of the human family and the earth. What could be more possible at the same time? We can cry out; we can name the pain. We can shout "*Stop!*" We want no more of guns and "might is right," no more father rule, no more "masculinity run amuck." Time for a change. The miracle of the oil pales in comparison to what might yet happen.

A Time Like This: Esther

The story of Esther claims to have its setting in the dispersion of Israel in Persia during the fifth century B.C.E. In fact, the background of Esther is more likely the situation of severe persecution under Antiochus Epiphanes in Palestine during the second century B.C.E. Esther takes place a long time after the period of the Judges, when the nation's life has once again become fragile and endangered. Esther's context is the royal court at times narrowed to the harem, where she is cut off from access to information and to possible participation in the life of her people.

Though the actual background of the book is somber and life-threatening, the tone of the text is often mocking, especially in the description of the oppressors. The king, Ahasuerus, is the picture of the gullible, ignorant administrator, wax in the hands of clever and unscrupulous advisers. Haman is the petty tyrant, dangerous when provoked, full of himself, busy manipulating the king to achieve his ends. Mockery, thumbing one's nose at the oppressor, laughter, are natural defense mechanisms under oppression and may actually serve as a means for survival. The constant partying in Esther reinforces the mocking tenor of the book. But every time there is a party, death hides around the corner.

The story, set in Persia of the fifth century B.C.E., is certainly not based on historical events. While this is a well-documented period, customs as described in Esther are unknown. Other descriptions are extremely untenable. The story is more a folktale than history, a tale in which the weak outdo the strong and the wicked work their own undoing, a story that evokes a smile which makes life bearable under violent persecution. The tie to the history of the Jewish people in the sense of their existence under this persecution is real enough, alas. Another historical link, in contrast, is the celebration of life and survival as manifested in the Jewish festival of Purim.

When I was in first or second grade, I had a close friend who lived a few miles outside our village, which meant spending time at her house if we wanted to play together. My friend's family lived on an elaborate farm with abundant space for playing, the ride to and from her house was a pleasant one, and the visits should have been ideal. What made them somewhat of a nightmare for me were the rumors that went around about this family. They were Jehovah's Witnesses. There were not many people belonging to this group in our region, and some mystery surrounded it. This was not what created my nightmare. What frightened me during the visits was the idea people were spreading that the Jehovah's Witnesses practiced child sacrifice. The rumors about this were persistent. Here was a group of people who dared to be different. Why, they must be strange people, they were seen . . . bzzz . . . bzzz . . . bzzz. Tongues wagged, stories were created, and I took them seriously, knowing no better. What was meant as a malicious rumor to make people's lives difficult had direct and life-threatening potential for me. With what terror did I watch my friend's mother wield her knives in the kitchen in preparation for her meals! If they did it once, they could do it again, and who was to say that I might not be the next child? All this was real enough and frightening enough for me. It was probably even more real and threatening to my friend's family, who had rumors like these spread about them and who were shunned by the community. All they had done was to have an allegiance to a community that created a difference for them. This difference was intolerable to others. They were different, so they must be wicked. Much like this and worse, the Jews were considered in the Christian countries in which they were dispersed. They, too, were commonly accused of child sacrifice in medieval Europe and were held to be guilty of monstrous crimes, including the spread of the bubonic plague.

"There is a people," said Haman to the king, "whose laws are different" (Esth. 3:8). And do you know what, King? They are all over the place! And do you know what else? They do not obey the laws! Criminals is what they are! I ask you: Are these people fit to live? And the king does not need to hear more. The Jews must die. Their sin is that they have set themselves apart. It enraged Haman, the tyrant, who had to have the whole world under his control. Dislike of difference can easily grow into fear and hatred. Recent studies have pointed to the fact that there may be profound differences between women and men that cause different approaches to life, differences, says Carol Gilligan, that in themselves are not a problem.[7] The problem arises because one of the approaches to life, the male one, has been made the norm, and by this norm the behavior of the other sex is measured. If women are different, they must be lower; if they are different, they must be less smart—they must be dangerous! Or the norm may result in the contrasting judgment that women's difference causes them to be higher, more tender, more caring, and more peaceful; women must be saints! Either image, that of wicked seductress or saint, is confining and oppressive, insofar as the image arises from a male perspective that sets the standard for sainthood as well as depravity.

In the story of Esther, Esther represents a difference on three levels: as a woman, as a stranger, and as a Jew. As a stranger, she is at greater risk than those who are at home in the land. As a Jew, a member of a persecuted minority, she is even more vulnerable, and her life will be forfeit once the decree against the Jews is put into effect. As a woman, she seems to have power, since she is called a queen. Her royal power is, however, set against the backdrop of the disappearance of Queen Vashti, who was banished for a minor offense. In fact, a woman like Esther is more isolated than most women, without access to public information or to the possibility of playing a role on behalf of her people. Her silence regarding her ties to the Jews (Esth. 2:20), while it lessens the danger, reinforces her weakness. Esther, in the harem, does not know of the impending doom of the Jews.

When our episode opens, Mordecai, Esther's cousin and former guardian, who has stayed in touch with her, is about to let her know what is happening. The scene takes place in and around the palace harem, with the servants acting as go-betweens.

> Mordecai got to know all that had been done, so Mordecai tore his clothes, dressed in sack and ashes, and went out into the midst of the city, crying loudly and bitterly. He went up to the entrance of Kingsgate, for no one might enter Kingsgate dressed in a sack. And in every province, wherever the king's command

> and his decree was announced, there was great lamentation among the Jews; sack and ashes were the bed of many.
>
> Then came Esther's maids and eunuchs, and they told her. So the queen became very frightened, and she sent clothes to dress Mordecai, so he might put his sack aside, but he did not accept. So Esther called Hatak, a royal eunuch appointed to her, and commanded him concerning Mordecai, to find out what this was all about. Hatak went out to Mordecai, to the city square in front of Kingsgate.
>
> And Mordecai told him all that befell him and also the sum of money that Haman had said to pay into the king's coffers for the Jews and their destruction. Also, the copy of the written decree, issued in Susa for their destruction, he gave to him to show Esther, and to tell her and urge her to go to the king, to implore and beseech him on account of her people. Hatak came and told Esther Mordecai's words.
>
> Esther 4:1–9

Esther's first reaction to Mordecai's behavior is fear; her first activity is an attempt to stop his behavior. Her reaction is interesting. She might well have acted this way had she known of the doom of the Jews. The next verse, however, reveals that she had no such knowledge, for she sends her servant to "find out what this was all about." Although he acts on his own, Mordecai is here presented as a participant in an activity of his entire community: lamentation over what is to befall them is shared by all the Jews. In contrast, Esther reacts in a fashion that reveals her isolation. Up to this point, Esther has not told anyone that she is Jewish, on Mordecai's advice (Esth. 2:20). It is publicly known, on the other hand, that Mordecai is a Jew, from his altercation with Haman (Esth. 3:4–6). Is Esther fearful that she will be revealed as a Jew when the connection between Mordecai and herself becomes more widely known? Or is she fearful that the disturbance caused by Mordecai will cause him harm? In this kingdom of easy banishments, precarious celebrations and hangings, who knows what repercussions unexplained behavior may cause! The text does not provide the reason for Esther's fear. The effect of the description is that she comes across as one who is not in the know, who relies on her servants to build the bridge of communication between herself and the outside world, and who is anything but resolute.

Mordecai is the one who acts and speaks with determination. He refuses to change his behavior; he speaks full of knowledge and direction. The information he gives to Hatak is exact and detailed. His request to Esther clusters words of supplication together: tell her, urge her, go, implore, beseech. There is no doubt that Mordecai knows what he wants and why he wants it. His earlier directives to Esther about her identity are to be disregarded in view of the urgency of the moment.

> Esther charged Hatak to tell Mordecai the following: "All the servants of the king and the people in the royal provinces know that if anyone, man or woman, enters into the royal courtyard without an invitation, one law applies: they are killed, unless the king stretches out his scepter of gold to them. Then they live. As for me, I have not been invited to enter the king's presence for these thirty days." So they told Mordecai Esther's words.
>
> Mordecai said to return to Esther the following reply: "Do not imagine that, because you are in the royal household, you will save your life, unlike the rest of the Jews! For if you are silent at this time, escape and deliverance will arise for the Jews from elsewhere, but you and your father's house will perish. And who knows whether you have not come to the kingdom for a time like this?"
>
> Esther said to return to Mordecai the following reply: "Go, gather all the Jews in Susa and fast on my account; do not eat or drink for three days, night and day. I also will fast with my maids. Then I will go to the king against the law. If I perish, I perish."
>
> Mordecai left and did according to all that Esther had charged him.
>
> Esther 4:10–17

The second half of the chapter shifts the tone by directly reporting speech. This shift heightens the tensions and sharpens the focus on the different characters. Up to this moment, Esther has been a dependent. Her dependence on her cousin was emphasized in the text, which states several times that her relationship to Mordecai was that of a daughter (Esth. 2:7,15) and that she did as Mordecai told her (Esth. 2:10,20). It comes as a shock, then, to hear her utter what amounts to a refusal of Mordecai's request: "All the servants . . . and the people . . . know." Does Mordecai not know? It is ironic that Esther, who is the one in ignorance, should be the one to reveal knowledge. She had always done as Mordecai told her, and what now is her position? The king chose her as his new queen, but apparently her powers of attraction have waned. He has not asked for her for a month. She, who walks on shifting, unsafe ground, has reason to know the laws of the palace, and she knows that it would mean risking her life if she went uninvited into the presence of the king. And what good would this be to her people? Esther's tone is almost sarcastic. She is out of favor or forgotten. Does Mordecai not know this? Does he realize what he is asking her to do?

Mordecai's reply is direct and matter-of-fact. Esther will die anyway; in fact, she might die while her people survive. Twice, Mordecai indicates the time as one of great urgency: "This time . . . a time like this" (Esth. 4:14). The moment has arrived for Esther when she must decide to be active or to let the events overcome her. In either case, the outcome for herself may be bleak. Mordecai does not offer her a great deal of hope, but he offers her a choice.

Such words as Mordecai's, though they may not be kind, have the effect of shocking someone into facing reality. Esther, in her final reply, is able to give this reality a name. She will be involved in civil disobedience—"I will go to the king against the law"—but she will go in full knowledge of the risk involved: "If I perish, I perish."

Esther's initial refusal serves to wrest her character out of its dependent status so that her acceptance of the task can take place in the context of her new maturity. For the first time in the exchange, she is the subject of active verbs: I will fast, I will go, I perish. Her task she will have to do alone, in her own way. She does not ask Mordecai for instructions; in a telling reversal of roles, she is the one to give him direction. Significantly, the entire episode is framed by the words "Esther charged," emphasizing the change in one who entered the scene "very frightened."

"A time like this" indicates the moment of urgency that demands a choice. The choice is not so much between success and failure as between passivity and activity, between letting things happen and making them happen. "A time like this" is the moment when it is up to us to decide whether we step in on behalf of the possibility of life. The stakes are high and the future is uncertain, but only as people who see the situation for what it is, who are able to give it its proper name, can we become participants in the mediation for life. Knowing the facts, in the face of oppression, women face the choice. They can choose to be silent, or they can choose to speak and act, at high risk and though they may perish in either case. Words and action will be based on the slender "who knows?"

Esther's immediate context is the harem, which I interpret as symbolic for the home environment that keeps certain women protected, safe, and well cared for, yet at the same time can leave them isolated, ignorant, and dependent. The harem is the place where we are "queen," where the bills are paid and there is someone to stand between us and the world outside. Our attractiveness, like Esther's attractiveness, assures us of an abiding place there. The family is the one place where women have exercised power. This power is often pointed to as matriarchal and is therefore used as an argument against the need for liberation of women from the structures as they are. The problem is that power exercised within these narrow confines is a sham, as Esther's power was a sham, which warps both women and their environment. The exchange between Mordecai and Esther shows that the imagined safety of the harem is a sham also. Esther appears "frightened," and Mordecai points out that her life is in grave danger even if she prefers not to step out of the harem. The screen between ourselves in the harem and the world is thin, and we are, in this assumed safety, only one man away from poverty.

Esther's larger context is that of the Jewish people, persecuted and in danger of being destroyed. Their difference has made them, in the end, so vulnerable in this kingdom that their lives are not safe. Esther has kept this difference at a distance by hiding her Jewish identity. But in the end, it is in claiming this identity that she finds the strength to do what the moment requires. Women's larger context is formed by poor women, by all women who suffer from oppression because of race and class, whose difference is putting them in danger of their lives. In claiming our identity, we look in the direction of those among us who suffer the most, who determine what it means to be women in a patriarchal world. In claiming our identity in this larger context, we can find the strength both to embrace our difference and to advocate change.

Acting as mature persons does not mean that we proceed in an isolated autonomy. Esther requests of Mordecai that her people share her fast. By this request, she draws her community around her symbolically. Esther is on her way out from the community that isolates her in her difference, the harem; on the way out, and as part of her move, she claims her alliance with her proper community and thus embraces her difference as being on the outside of the harem. She asks that her people accompany her symbolically in her preparation for the intercession to come. This alliance creates both for herself and her community new opportunities for strength and hope. Esther takes a stand with her decision on the side of her difference, her self. As a woman in her best clothes, as a stranger, as a Jew, uninvited, she goes to stand before the king. He has the power to decide whether she lives or dies, but he has lost the power to set the norm for Esther's approach to life.

Three Stories

Who are we? How shall we live? Where is God? We women are defined by our connections to men through marriage or blood ties; we are expected to behave in ways that welcome and nourish even the oppressor. We are dependent and poor; our children die, or they are taken from our arms. We have only a role to play within the narrow confines of our family, where we are protected and kept unaware of the reality of other women's lives. All these aspects the biblical text confirms. On the other hand, the text sets us free to participate, to step out of our tent, to break out of the harem of our ignorance and pretended safety in order to seek our proper alliances with the victims of oppressive structures and to stand with them, on their side, God's side. We are those called to stand on God's side, to raise our voice against oppression, to work for liberation, and to name our pain and others' pain. Patriarchy as idolatry is not operating in these texts. The power of men over women is limited and changeable. One sees here, rather, the shattering of the idol and the possibility for women to live out their calling as God's free people.

5

Reformed and Feminist

By the time of the Reformation, the church had become so warped by human custom that nothing but a total overhaul would save it from its idolatrous and destructive path, according to the Reformers. The authority for this change they sought in the Bible. The search for the authoritative word of God offered no safe solutions. It underscored, rather, the need for a radical transformation of what had become misformed in the church.

If today the church, including the Reformed church, has become warped by the idolatry of patriarchy, another radical reformation may be needed. We have asked whether the institutional church is capable of supporting a new community of women and men. The texts we have studied provide a strong impulse and authority for change of the existing situation. Until now, we have looked at the pervasive presence of patriarchy in the structures of the world of today and yesterday. We have noted how the church participates in patriarchal structures in a general way. It remains for us to uncover the specific features of the face of patriarchy in churches with a Reformed heritage. In this context, we will look again to the biblical text as founding authority not only of the reformation of the past but for the change to come.

An Absence of Women

One of the most famous paintings of the crucifixion of Jesus was done in the early sixteenth century by Mathias Grünewald. Called the Isenheim Altarpiece, it consists of a series of panels on the life and death of Jesus. These panels were displayed above the church altar at appropriate times of the liturgical year. Today, the painting is located in a museum that was once a monastery chapel, in Colmar, France. I visited the museum because I especially wanted to see the paintings. Its fame is due partly to the panel on which John the Baptist points an index finger of disproportionate size at the figure of Jesus. I had come prepared to admire this gesture of John the Baptist. It was, however, not the Baptist, or his finger, or yet the crucified Christ, appallingly realistic though it is in the portrayal of its agony, that fixed my attention. What took my breath away was the depiction of two figures at the foot of the cross: Mary, the mother of Jesus, and Mary Magdalene. About these women, who witness the death of a son and a teacher, there is nothing stylized, nothing decorous. Their mouths are twisted with grieving, and their hands writhe in anguish. Never had I seen the grief over the death of Jesus portrayed so eloquently. Neither had I been made so aware of the presence of women at the crucifixion.

Grünewald, who worked at the beginning of the Protestant Reformation, painted for the Roman Catholic Church, a church which long used sculpture and painting as "books for the laity," to impart knowledge of the biblical story to those for whom the text was not available. Since such representations were judged to be idolatrous by the Protestant Reformers, the only acceptable representation of God's presence and of the biblical story in the Protestant churches became entirely verbal. One result of this change was that women were no longer a significant part of this representation. Besides the veneration of the Virgin Mary, the Roman Catholic tradition acknowledged many women saints who were included in the life of worship. With the Protestant Reformation, these women disappeared from worship in the churches who joined the Reformation. The Reformation thus brought about, perhaps unintentionally, a masculinization of the world of faith. The focus on language, entirely masculine in its references to God, gave a masculine cast to the expressions of faith and worship. It was the absence of women and the significance of their presence that the Isenheim Altarpiece brought to my awareness. I had known that there were women present at the crucifixion, from the unanimous witness of the Gospel accounts. I had even taken note of the fact. But the power of that reality had never before had the impact it did when I faced the Grünewald painting.

The masculinization of the expression of the Christian faith in the Protestant churches was reinforced through the male hierarchy of these churches. Even though Calvin had declared that the notion of hierarchy is unbiblical, the Reformation created a hierarchy by its very emphasis on the Bible and on a clergy trained in interpreting the text on the basis of the original languages. The laity was controlled in its hearing of the word of God by those who interpreted that word for them:

> Once they had smashed the images and altars and chased away the priests . . . the laity once again found themselves restricted from above. They may have had a new kind of piety, but it was a carefully formulated and clearly dictated piety. More than had been the case before, religious expression began to be controlled from above, by the pastors and consistories.[1]

Of course, these bodies were, until a very short time ago, exclusively male. It is true that in the Roman Catholic Church before the Reformation the clerical hierarchy was male also. But during the long ages of its existence, there were many women who were able to provide leadership of their own, especially through convent life. Not until the late twentieth century are women leaders and interpreters found in significant numbers in the life of the churches with a Reformed heritage.

Recently, when on sabbatical leave in France, I took a class in Old Testament. The subject of the class was the story cycle, in Genesis 12–25, concerning Israel's ancestors. The title of the course was "The Abraham Cycle."

One morning I find myself looking at the teacher, who stands in front of the blackboard on which he has written names from Genesis 11:31: *Terah, Abram, Lot, Sarah.* He points to the first three and says, "Father, son, grandson." This listing obviously leaves Sarah out of the conversation. When someone remarks on this, he observes, "Well, women were less important." The class giggles nervously, at which he shrugs and says, "Well, that's the way it is." Later, in pointing out the importance of genealogies in the book of Genesis, our teacher puts the names of people with a genealogy on the board as well. The board is now filled with names, all of them male. Except for Sarah. She is there, but the teacher does not know what to do with her, and she is in any case one of the women, who were "less important." Since Sarah is there, especially in view of the lesser importance of women, she must have some importance, even if it is "less." Our teacher does not get to discuss this lesser importance, and so, in reality, Sarah has no importance; she does not count. Because the teacher generalized his remark, he has erased, along with Sarah, all other women from the text and from the world of faith. This is ultimately the message that comes through to a class filled with women and men preparing for ministry in congregations that will often consist of 90 percent women. Women are not important; they do not count. Congregations will receive this message from one who knows, from a teacher who has the authority to tell the students "the way it is."

But, one might protest, that is not what the teacher meant to do. He meant to say that Terah, Abram, and Lot have more importance in the text than Sarah. Even from a superficial view, however, this is not true. Sarah has certainly greater importance in terms of text devoted to her than Terah and also than Lot. More lines are spent on Sarah than on those two combined. She has a dominant role in the family, and she is crucial to the unfolding of God's promise, according to God (cf. Gen. 17:15–21). In view of the patriarchal cast of the text it is, in fact, rather remarkable that Sarah is accorded so much attention. It is the contemporary patriarchal bias that erases her from the text.

The evening after the class, I listened to a public lecture at the Protestant seminary. During this lecture, the speaker remarked that the faith community has need of turning its attention to history. "For," he said, "it is by looking back that we are able to orient ourselves to the present, and to prepare ourselves for the future." This remark, which seemed an appropriate one, caused me to ponder what it might mean to look back and see no one there. According to the speaker, disorientation and an inability to meet the future would result. Yet women have lived with their absence in history for a long time. Not only have women lived thus, but men have lived with the absence of women as well. If men, in looking back, see only men active in history, they also look at an absence that must cause disorientation in them, too. It is time this absence was filled in the Christian community, for certainly women were present in history, and also in biblical history. Always and of utmost importance is the question regarding women's presence in the text. Without this presence women, and the community of women and men, cannot acquire a sense of identity and can design no way to meet the future.

In returning to the position of a student, it became once more clear to me how much authority the word of a teacher carries and how easy it is to accept that word on the basis of the teacher's authority. Teaching and learning in partnership is a difficult thing. The old male hierarchies need to be challenged from above and below, by teacher and by student, so that both will become involved in the process of learning and teaching. Such a process should take into account that teachers bring the advantage of the accumulated knowledge of their life experience to the same endeavor. In the study of the Bible, such a process would enhance the knowledge of all involved, while it would militate against passing on knowledge as an exercise in domination and perpetuation of oppressive worldviews. In fact, regarding the Bible, such a process would approach more closely the Reformed ideal of the accessibility of the biblical text for all believers.

A Presence of Women

I have said that there must be two conditions for the Bible to function as God's Word: We must have something to ask, and we must expect to hear something. These are also the basic principles of Bible study. These two, question and expectation, form the starting point. When we ask about women's presence in the text and press on with our questions, we are doing more than looking back. We look to the text for guidance, for authentication, and for redemption of our experience. These two, authentication and redemption, are the goal of Bible study. This goal is not a finish line. It is more like a moment which may occur and reoccur. Studying the Bible is a process with which we are never finished. Just as we do not know ahead of time what God's Word may be for us in the text, so is there always still another word waiting.

In our questioning, we listen to voices that have not been heard from before. These are our own voices, the voices of women who, for the first time in history, ask questions of the Bible as women, questions that arise out of their experience and that, for the first time in history, are raised publicly. These are also and especially the voices of women who experience discrimination and oppression in multiple ways because they come from groups other than those of the privileged classes in the industrialized world. We listen to Elsa Tamez's questions as she explores the texts in Genesis that concern Hagar. We listen to Renita Weems as she considers the role of Queen Vashti in the Esther story. Questions and responses from women who come from the most deprived groups among us reveal the significance of women who are on the periphery of the biblical text and interpretative concerns. Hagar and Sarah both are present in the text in a significant way. Vashti has an important role to play in the story of Esther. By listening to the voices of women from marginalized groups, we may begin to hear the voices from these same groups in the text.

If it is true that the iconoclastic spirit of Calvinism is aimed at building up rather than tearing down, then such an iconoclastic spirit might well have to take hold of those who look toward a reformation of male dominance in the church. The movement toward this renewed whitewashing of the churches needs to have both the character of "turning from" and "turning toward."

The first step, the "turning from," is repentance. Repentance is traditionally of crucial importance for a community when it needs to move in a new direction. According to the biblical records, words and acts of repentance accompanied such reforms as those of Kings Hezekiah and Josiah in Judah before the Babylonian exile (2 Kings 22:11,19; 2 Chron. 34:19–27). After the exile, the reform of Ezra was preceded by powerful expressions of repentance (cf. Ezra 9:3–15). Furthermore, according to the unanimous report of the Synoptic Gospels, John the Baptist preached repentance in preparation for the arrival of the Christ (Matt. 3:2; Mark 1:4; Luke 3:3). Repentance will indicate the seriousness with which the church views the wounds it has inflicted by the perpetuation and upholding of patriarchy; repentance will indicate also the degree of earnestness with which the church looks to the possibility of representing more closely the new humanity in Christ. Without repentance, the vision of the promised land will be a far-off and unreachable ideal, an illusion rather than a realizable vision. Without repentance, the turn from the old ways of being the church, there can be no turn toward the new way of being.

The entire community must engage in repentance because patriarchal ideology and structures are harmful to both women and men, but in different ways. Men are harmed by patriarchy from being the dominators, women from being the dominated. This difference will create a different context for repentance, but it does not take away from the fact that repentance must be engaged in by the whole church, not just by some in the church. Each group contributes to the structures of oppression from its place of participation. Those who belong to the dominating group repent of their domination that destroys life and prevents the new creation from coming into being. Those who are dominated repent of their silence, their lack of protest in the face of oppression, and their refusal to build alliances on behalf of those who suffer most. All repent of their cooperation in hindering the advent of the new creation.[2]

Once the community of the faithful has taken the step of repentance, it can begin to turn toward the new creation of male and female made possible in Christ. This turn toward the new way of being, the promised land, will need to take place on all levels of the church's existence, the practical as well as the theoretical, the symbolic as well as the actual. The presence of women in the community of the church will need to become a reality. This turn toward a new community will mean a rethinking and rewording of the symbolic representation of God. Language that liberates, rather than language that limits and imprisons, needs to be found to represent God and people. On all levels of the work to be done, the biblical text needs to be the central and authoritative inspiration, not in the sense that the Bible offers blueprints but in the sense that through its words the Spirit of God inspires the community to live more closely in the image of God and less as a mirror of the culture.

Specifically, we in the Reformed communities need to address the abuses brought about in the wake of the Protestant

Reformation. This will involve a cleansing of the masculinization of the church on all levels of its existence. Women will be called into presence in the church through a careful study of the biblical text and a new accessibility to the Bible. This study will involve exposing the patriarchal bias of the biblical text as the "lisp of God." We need to note carefully the new approaches to the biblical text and the new translations from both women and men intent on changing the relations between female and male. Certain questions should receive attention regarding every text: Who are the women present in the text? How are they present? What do they say? How do they act? What is the result of the presence of women in the text? How do we integrate the fact that, in a text, women are absent and only men are heard and seen? The identity of the new community can only grow if such questions are faithfully pursued, for only thus will the questions that lie at the basis of all our questions take shape and receive response.

An Alliance of Women

From the early stages of my life came the insight that members of dominated groups must band together to form a crucial alliance on behalf of structural change and liberation. I also learned that such alliances are not easily forged, that once made they are fragile, and that powerful forces set up and maintain barriers that keep groups without power divided. Since there is risk in such alliances, fear and desire for self-preservation may be one of the barriers. Also, small privileges (in reality illusions of freedom and change) may be accorded to one group and not the other; such privileges are treasured by the group that possesses them and resented by the groups that do not. Thus, all levels of the society or organization stay in place, and no movement toward true liberation and change is possible. The barriers of division are maintained by those who have a vested interest in preventing change and by those who passively consent to this interest.

Women are kept divided from each other in this way and are thus prevented from making the alliances that will bring about change in relations between the sexes. Unless women of all races, ages, religions, and classes are able to form a community for change, their newfound presence in the structures of church and society will be a token presence, hiding the true reality of their absence. Unless women form these alliances in the church, calling the church to repentance and change, women will be made to fit into the patriarchal structures as they are without being able to change those structures.

The most fitting biblical paradigm of women's alliance across barriers of culture and age is that of Ruth and Naomi. For them, models for alliance were even less available than they are for women today. Their world, as reflected in the story, is defined by the authority of the male. Set within the framework of uncertain economic provisions—the immediate background is famine (see Ruth 1:1)—there are first three men to surround the one woman, Naomi, then two men to secure the state of three women, Naomi and her daughters-in-law. The presence of the men assures the physical and psychological well-being of this small group. Soon, however, the balance tips in the other direction, as the men die and the three women are left behind, unprotected, without a single male to stand between them and the renewed threat of starvation. Economically, socially, and psychologically, these women are the first on the list of those who need help, in ancient Israel no less than today. Naomi is not just making empty sounds when she points out to her daughters-in-law her inability to provide them with husbands (1:11).

There is indeed little hope for Naomi and those with her as they stand arguing on the Moab–Judah road. By clinging to her, the younger women only share in the lack of hope that is part of Naomi's future. Naomi looks back, and what she sees is the presence of men: safety. This orients her to the present, and what she sees is the presence of women: vulnerability. Past safety and present vulnerability do not open up a future for her. Her plans for the future are to go back home alone and to stare at the safe past. Naomi is a realist; she sees the situation for what it is, she knows the facts and that she cannot change these facts. The statistics are devastating; a vast complex of social customs and laws holds her and the young women prisoners to their female status, a subordinate, deprived, and ultimately endangered status without the presence of men. Only if these two, Orpah and Ruth, go "home" (i.e., if they find another man) will they have any kind of future. And this is what she hopes for them when she says, "May the Lord grant you rest, each in her husband's house" (Ruth 1:9). Finally, one of the women obeys her; Orpah goes home, bowing to the facts and fitting herself into them. The other woman refuses to go. Ruth disobeys Naomi and speaks words to her that are so fraught with meaning and depth that they have the effect of silencing the older woman (Ruth 1:16–17).

In this way Ruth, in her impossible circumstances, creates for Naomi an opening. Their partnership, Ruth and Naomi's, does not begin as a sharing. It is Ruth who takes the initiative and who shows the particular qualities that finally make the alliance successful, one in which each can participate according to her ability.

The first quality Ruth exhibits is that for which Naomi had already praised her and her sister-in-law, Orpah. In Hebrew *hesed,* in our English versions often translated as "lovingkindness" or simply "kindness," it is the quality that marks the relation of the God of Israel to God's people. I prefer the translation "devotion," in the sense that this word conveys the dedicated, complete loyalty that is intended. The God of Israel is the God who is devoted, who shows devotion to Israel and to all humanity. In God's alliance with Israel and the world, God shows a preference for the weakest and the most oppressed. In God's alliance with Israel at the time of the Exodus, God "clings" to the weakest and most oppressed group around. God's people are called on to show the same behavior toward one another that God shows to them. The life of *hesed* is what marks the people of God. To Ruth, devotion means that she refuses to abandon this hopeless woman, Naomi, to her life without a future.

> "Do not ask me to leave you, to turn from following you. For where you go, I go; where you sleep, I sleep; your people, my people; your God, my God. Where you die, I die, and there I will be buried. Thus may the Lord do to me, yes more, if even death will separate me from you"
>
> Ruth 1:16–17

We know Ruth's words from the wedding ceremony, of course. And that is ironic, for the relationship between Ruth and Naomi is not at all like a marriage, and their situation could not be more unlike a wedding; one might say that it is precisely the lack of a wedding that produces Ruth's speech.

What is present in the text? Two women, two persons of the same gender, who lack the status, the power, and the resources to survive, are bound into an alliance when one of them goes against the stated wishes of the other. Ruth joins herself to the least promising person in her environment, a person who, by her own admission, will not be able to provide for her. Ruth turns the world upside down by refusing to break with Naomi and by "clinging" to her as if she were as valuable as a husband. She adds her own weakness to Naomi's, as if that would make for strength!

It won't work! How often have we heard that? How much have women internalized this remark? Women don't like each other, they don't work well together, they need a leader, a senior pastor, a man in the house! Even though we may know better, and we have observed how well women's organizations have worked, we may still doubt that we can do it when push comes to shove. Women's presence, after all, does not count. Congregations that consist of a very high percentage of women are no congregations at all in our minds. That must be Naomi's way of thinking, for she does not seem open to the promise of Ruth's presence for her own life. "Full did I go," Naomi says to her neighbors on her return to Bethlehem, "empty the Lord brings me back." "Empty"—of the devoted woman at her side, Naomi says not a word. To Naomi, Ruth is not there. She in no sense fills Naomi's emptiness. "Call me Dour, not Delight," she cries (Ruth 1:19–21). Ruth acts out her devotion against her environment, against Naomi's objections, and finally against Naomi's denial of her supportive presence. In Naomi's eyes, Ruth does not count. Such total dedication as Ruth's may well be necessary if women are to make the alliances that are needed.

Ruth's second quality may be difficult for women to embrace. It is a quality with which many of us are ill at ease. The Hebrew word *hayil* connotes strength and power, most often in connection with men, especially of prowess in battle. On the rare occasions that the word is used of women in the Bible, the translators tend to shade the word differently, using "virtue" or "worth" (see Prov. 31:10; Ruth 3:11). Strength, power, or valor are words we might use to translate the *hayil* that Ruth exhibits in her alliance with Naomi, a quality that enables her to see things through, to do what is difficult and risky, to push at the boundaries of existence, and to extend the possibilities. As her devotion is most visible at the moment when she refuses to abandon Naomi, so her valor becomes most clear when she goes to glean and when she meets Boaz, who is himself introduced in the story as a man of *hayil*:

> Naomi had a kinsman, actually of her husband's, a powerful and wealthy man, of Elimelech's family, whose name was Boaz. Ruth, the Moabite, said to Naomi, "Let me go to the field, and glean grain behind someone in whose eyes I find favor." She said to her, "Go, my daughter." So she went and came and gleaned in the field behind the harvesters and as luck would have it, she happened to be on the plot of land that belonged to Boaz of Elimelech's family.
>
> Ruth 2:1–3

Luck is the writer's ironic word for the helping hand of God. Something that may almost escape our attention in the episode that follows is the apparent risk of molestation and harassment that people such as Ruth faced when they worked as gleaners. She has put herself in charge of the economic sustenance of her small family of two, and she does so at some risk. Boaz has to admonish his servants not "to shame her." He gives her extra food and tells his servants not to scold her. Naomi, at Ruth's return, remarks that in staying with Boaz's workers Ruth will avoid being molested elsewhere (2:9, 15–16, 22). These observations must necessarily lead to the conclusion that harassment and molestation were not rare occurrences.

Finally, Naomi becomes aware of the possibilities of life, at least for Ruth, and she formulates a plan. Boaz has shown great kindness to Ruth, but he could play a more important role yet. He was actually in line to be a redeemer to Naomi and Ruth. Redeemers were those males in ancient Israel who were appointed by custom and law to ease the economic burden of the destitute among their relatives. When the harvest ends and Ruth's gleaning days are over, lack of security still looms large for the two women. Their concern is the restoration of security on all levels, which can only happen through a fortuitous marriage. To open up this possibility, Naomi sends Ruth to the threshing floor. Through Ruth's presence, Naomi has gained a new sense of herself, as a clever woman full of resources. She generates the idea of the visit to the threshing floor and launches Ruth into her next encounter with Boaz. Naomi assumes that Boaz will take the lead, and thus she instructs Ruth: "He will tell you what you should do" (Ruth 3:4). But it is, in the end, Ruth who will tell Boaz what to do. She goes down to the threshing floor and from then on acts on her own lights:

> In the middle of the night, the man shivered, groped around and—look!—a woman was lying at his feet! He said to her, "Who are you?" She said, "I am Ruth, your servant; spread your wings over me for you are a redeemer." He said, "Blessed may you be by the Lord, my daughter; you have done a second deed of devotion better than the first. . . . All that you ask I will do, since all my people know that you are a woman of valor"
>
> Ruth 3:8–11

Boaz recognizes her worth, and it is from his mouth that the praise comes of her devotion and power. Ruth's valor, her *hayil,* consists above all in her willingness to call the person in charge on his responsibilities. It is not enough to be kind; it is not enough to be religious. A true change can only come about by a radical turn. To such a turn she calls Boaz. An older man has to act as a young man, a kind man has to become a lover, and a respected citizen has to bargain in public for his wife.

There are many kind men in our surroundings. They try hard to ease the burdens that they see women carry. They are concerned because they face the pain of women and feel that they have contributed to this pain. Not infrequently, such men also feel helpless, and they express this helplessness through anger. Why can't women see how hard they are trying to be helpful, and be more appreciative of their efforts? For Ruth and Naomi, as well as for women today, kindness and understanding on the part of men are necessary and appreciated, but they are only a beginning. If nothing else follows, deprivation and lack of security are still the order of the day. We need a turn of events, a radical change, the kind of eye-opener that Judah and Boaz received, to begin life out of a sense of the new humanity.

In the end, Ruth and Boaz are married, and they have a son. The story could have ended there, and it would have been a good end, an end that is also the beginning of a new sequence of events, of God's involvement with Israel and the world through King David and Jesus Christ. The change begun on the threshing floor finds it culmination in the Redeemer, through whom we are a new creation. The word "redeemer" spoken by Ruth on the threshing floor sets up echoes in the history of faith.

At the city gate, (see Ruth 4:1–12) the patriarchal cast of the story is strongly evident; for the first time in this story, men are the central characters of the narrative. But the story of Ruth and Naomi continues:

> Then the women said to Naomi, "Blessed be the Lord who has not withheld a redeemer from you today. May his name be blessed in Israel. He shall be to you a life-restorer and a provider in your old age, for your daughter-in-law who loves you has borne him, and she is better to you than seven sons!"
>
> Ruth 4:14–15

The women of the community, first considered to be of no use by Naomi, come back to the center. The presence of women has provided life for Naomi, whether she was in a mood to recognize it or not. The neighbor women, who surround Naomi as if they have never been absent from her, make important statements about God, the child, and Ruth. They praise Ruth extravagantly by pointing to her worth and by saying that she loves Naomi. Ruth, according to the last appraisal of her in the story, did not act in the first instance out of self-concern, nor out of concern for her dead husband, but was motivated by love for the woman next to her, who was not her age, her nationality, or her religion. She has not used the opportunity for marriage and her own reestablishment to cut herself off from Naomi; rather, she uses it as a new opportunity to open up life for Naomi:

> Then Naomi took the child, put it in her lap, and became his nurse. And the neighbor women gave him a name, saying, "A son has been born to Naomi!" And they named him Obed. He is the father of Jesse, the father of David.
>
> Ruth 4:17–18

Ruth 4:15 is the only place in the Bible where the word "love" is used of a relationship between women. The root in

Hebrew has strong connotations of loyalty and allegiance as well as of emotions and indicates a type of relationship apparently not commonly observed among women in Israel. Our culture fosters love between women no more than Israel's did. The presence of women supporting one another is often viewed as a sign of weakness rather than strength, a sign of lack of male presence rather than the significance of women's presence. It is therefore important that this quality of Ruth is mentioned after her marriage and the birth of her son. The extraordinary statement about Ruth's love for Naomi glows like a jewel hidden in the patriarchal cast of the biblical text.

Ruth was not aware, in her situation, that she was anything but an unknown Moabite woman whose name would not outlast her generation. She did not know that, by walking with Naomi in devotion, power, and love, she was on her way to the birthplace of the world's redeemer. She only knew where to begin and how to hold on. Letty Russell, in *Household of Freedom,* points out that in the new house of authority, where authority is marked by authorizing the inclusion of all persons as partners, you need "to begin where you are and learn to make a stand for freedom of your sisters and brothers and of yourself in that place. Begin where you are to build up the new house from the foundation of your own experience and actions."[3]

We must begin where we are so that we can begin to make a change in the way things are. The way things are is marked by the sin of patriarchy. If we want to change this, we need to take patriarchy and its ultimately destructive results seriously. We need to take ourselves and our capacities seriously. We cannot accommodate ourselves to patriarchal structures and ways of being and expect those structures to change. The way to begin the adventure of change is by the way we operate, by teaming up differently, together, against the odds, in devotion, in power, and in love.

Notes

Chapter 1

1. Frederick Buechner, *Telling the Truth: The Gospel as Tragedy, Comedy, and Fairy Tale* (New York: Harper & Row, 1977).

2. John Calvin, *Institutes of the Christian Religion,* tr. Ford Lewis Battles and ed. John T. McNeill, 2 vols. (Philadelphia: Westminster Press, 1960), 4.16.14.

Chapter 2

1. The expression comes from Calvin, who stated that Scripture came "from the very mouth of God by human ministry." See John Calvin, *Institutes of the Christian Religion,* tr. Ford Lewis Battles and ed. John T. McNeill, 2 vols. (Philadelphia: Westminster Press, 1960), 1.8.5.

2. *Institutes,* 1.7.2.

3. Charles Garside, Jr., *The Origins of Calvin's Theology of Music: 1536–1543* (Philadelphia: The American Philosophical Society, 1979), p. 33.

4. The Westminster Confession of Faith, 1.8.

5. In his *Institutes,* Calvin wrote, "For who even of slight intelligence does not understand that, as nurses commonly do with infants, God is wont in a measure to 'lisp' in speaking with us?" (1.13.1). The word Calvin used in Latin for "lisp" is *balbutio,* which means to speak with a lisp or stammer. The translation of the French word *bégayer* is tilted more in the direction of "stammer." It is clear that Calvin had in mind the sounds—either a repetition of simple words or merely sounds without words—that one makes to infants as indi-

cations of love and care. A satisfactory solution to the translation of *balbutio* is not easily found, since the word itself is only an approximation of what Calvin had in mind. "Prattle" or "babble" offer themselves as possible alternatives.

6. For an extensive discussion of Calvin's principle of accommodation, see Jack B. Rogers and Donald K. McKim, *The Authority and Interpretation of the Bible* (New York: Harper & Row, 1979), pp. 98–100. Also see Ford Lewis Battles, "God Was Accommodating Himself to Human Capacity," *Interpretation* 31/1 (January 1977): 19–38.

7. Kornelis H. Miskotte, *When the Gods Are Silent* (New York: Harper & Row, 1967), p. 159.

8. James Sanders, *Torah and Canon* (Minneapolis: Augsburg Fortress Press, 1972).

9. Anne Tyler, *The Accidental Tourist* (New York: Alfred A. Knopf, 1985), p. 189.

Chapter 3

1. Elizabeth Dodson Gray, *Patriarchy as a Conceptual Trap* (Wellesley, Mass.: Roundtable Press, 1982), p. 129.

2. Bride burnings are also known as dowry murders. They take place when a bride's dowry is considered inadequate by the husband or his family. See *The New York Times,* January 13, 1977, as discussed by Mary Daly in *Gyn/Ecology* (Boston: Beacon Press, 1978), pp. 114–115.

3. From the poem "With No Immediate Cause" in Ntozake Shange, *Nappy Edges* (New York: St. Martin's Press, 1978), p. 114.

4. Ruth Sidel, *Women and Children Last: The Plight of Poor Women in Affluent America* (New York: Penguin Books, 1987), p. 11.

5. See Sidel, pp. 3, 152–154; see also Randy Albeda, et al., *Mink Coats Don't Trickle Down: The Economic Attack on Women* (Boston: South End Press, 1986), p. 49.

6. Barbara Seaman and Gideon Seaman, *Women and the Crisis in Sex Hormones* (New York: Rawson Associates, 1977).

7. Penny Wise Budoff, *No More Menstrual Cramps and Other Good News* (New York: Penguin Books, 1981), p. 219.

8. Edward C. Lehman, Jr., *Women Clergy: Breaking Through Gender Barriers* (New Brunswick, N.J.: Transaction Publications, 1985).

9. Robert Alter, *The Art of Biblical Narrative* (New York: Basic Books, 1983), p. 9.

10. See Rosemary Radford Ruether, *New Woman, New Earth: Sexist Ideologies and Human Liberation* (New York: Harper & Row, 1978), and Gerda Lerner, *The Creation of Patriarchy* (New York: Oxford University Press, 1986).

11. Ruether, *New Woman, New Earth,* p. 9.

12. Gray, *Patriarchy,* p. 82.

13. Phyllis Byrd, "Images of Women in the Old Testament," in *Religion and Sexism,* ed. Rosemary Radford Ruether (New York: Simon & Schuster, 1974), p. 56.

14. See Phyllis Trible, *Texts of Terror* (Philadelphia: Fortress Press, 1984).

15. Byrd, "Images of Women," p. 57.

Chapter 4

1. "Masculinity run amuck" is George Edward's phrase describing Sodom and Gomorrah. See George Edward, *Gay/Lesbian Liberation: A Biblical Perspective* (New York: Pilgrim Press, 1984), p. 78.

2. Ruth Sidel, *Women and Children Last: The Plight of Poor Women in America* (New York: Penguin Books, 1987), p. 25.

3. I owe my use of the expression "the words to say it" directly to Bob Randolph, who quoted them and helped me locate them; they are from the title of a book by the French writer Marie Cardinal. See Marie Cardinal, *Les mots pour le dire* (Paris: Grasset, 1975).

4. Walter Bruggemann, *The Prophetic Imagination* (Philadelphia: Fortress Press, 1978), p. 22.

5. *Justice, Peace, and the Integrity of Creation,* a second draft document prepared for the World Convocation of the World Council of Churches in Seoul, Korea, March 6–12, 1990, p. 7.

6. *Justice, Peace, and the Integrity of Creation,* p. 8.

7. See Carol Gilligan, *In a Different Voice: Psychological Theory and Women's Development* (Cambridge, Mass.: Harvard University Press, 1982). Also see Jean Baker Miller, *Toward a New Psychology of Women* (Boston: Beacon Press, 1976, 1986) and Anne Wilson Schaef, *Women's Reality: An Emerging Female System in the White Male Society* (New York: Harper & Row, 1986).

Chapter 5

1. Carlos M. N. Eire, *War Against the Idols* (New York: Cambridge University Press, 1986), p. 317.

2. In a recent document produced for an ecumenical forum of Christian women in Europe, it is precisely such repentance that is called for: repentance for the church's participation in the structure of oppression; repentance for the church's hesitation in creating the possibility for women and men to participate equally in the life of the church; and repentance for the church's prevention of the possibility of new relationships between men and women, relationships that would enable the birth of a new humanity. See Marga Buhrig's recent address in *Unité Chrétienne,* 95 (August 1989): 86–91.

3. Letty Russell, *Household of Freedom: Authority in Feminist Theology* (Philadelphia: Westminster Press, 1988), p. 65.

Sources

Chapter 2: The Reformation and the Bible

Primary and secondary sources on John Calvin

Calvin, John. *Calvin's Commentaries: Old Testament.* 30 vols. Reprint. Grand Rapids: Wm. B. Eerdmans Publishing Co., 1948.

———. *Calvin's New Testament Commentaries.* Ed. David W. and Thomas F. Torrance. Grand Rapids: Wm. B. Eerdmans Publishing Co., 1971.

———. *Institutes of the Christian Religion.* Tr. Ford Lewis Battles and ed. John T. McNeill. 2 vols. Philadelphia: Westminster Press, 1960.

Davies, Rupert E. *The Problem of Authority in the Continental Reformers: A Study in Luther, Zwingli, and Calvin.* London: Epworth Press, 1946.

Forstman, H. Jackson. *Word and Spirit: Calvin's Doctrine of Biblical Authority.* Stanford, Calif.: Stanford University Press, 1962.

Kraus, Hans Joachim. "Calvin's Exegetical Principles." Tr. Keith Crim. In *Interpretation* 31/1 (January 1977): 8–18.

Rogers, Jack B., and Donald K. McKim. *The Authority and Interpretation of the Bible: An Historical Approach.* New York: Harper & Row, 1979.

Sources on the status of the Bible before the Reformation

Deanesly, Margaret. *The Lollard Bible, and Other Medieval Biblical Versions.* New York: Cambridge University Press, 1966.

MacGregor, Geddes. *A Literary History of the Bible: From the Middle Ages to the Present Day.* Nashville: Abingdon Press, 1968.

Sources on the authority of the Bible and iconoclasm

Crew, Phyllis Mack. *Calvinist Preaching and Iconoclasm in the Netherlands, 1544–1569.* New York: Cambridge University Press, 1978.

For further reading

Douglass, Jane Dempsey. *Women, Freedom, and Calvin.* Philadelphia: Westminster Press, 1985.

Harkness, Georgia. *John Calvin: The Man and His Ethics.* New York: Henry Holt, 1931.

Huber, Elaine C. *Women and the Authority of Inspiration: A Reexamination of Two Prophetic Movements from a Contemporary Feminist Perspective.* Lanham, Md.: University Press of America, 1985.

Chapter 3: Women and the Bible

Sources on the Bible as literature

Alter, Robert. *The Art of Biblical Narrative.* New York: Basic Books, 1981.

Berlin, Adele. *Poetics and Interpretation of Biblical Narrative.* Sheffield: Almond Press, 1983.

Fishbane, Michael. *Text and Texture: Close Readings of Selected Biblical Texts.* New York: Schocken Books, 1979.

Sources on the economic status of women

Albelda, Randy, et al. *Mink Coats Don't Trickle Down: The Economic Attack on Women and People of Color.* Boston: South End Press, 1986.

Bergmann, Barbara R. *The Economic Emergence of Women.* New York: Basic Books, 1988.

Hewlett, Sylvia Ann. *A Lesser Life: The Myth of Women's Liberation in America.* New York: Warner Books, 1986.

Kozol, Jonathan. *Rachel and Her Children: Homeless Families in America. New York: Crown Publishers, 1988.*

Lefkowitz, Rochelle, and Ann Withorn. *For Crying Out Loud.* New York: Pilgrim Press, 1986.

Presbyterian Church (U.S.A.). *All the Livelong Day: Women and Work.* A study paper with recommendations adopted by the 200th

General Assembly (1988) of the Presbyterian Church (U.S.A.). Louisville, Ky.: Presbyterian Church (U.S.A.), 1988.

Sources on patriarchy

Gray, Elizabeth Dodson. *Patriarchy as a Conceptual Trap.* Wellesley, Mass.: Roundtable Press, 1982.

Lerner, Gerda. *The Creation of Patriarchy.* New York: Oxford University Press, 1986.

Ruether, Rosemary Radford. *Sexism and God-talk: Toward a Feminist Theology.* Boston: Beacon Press, 1983.

———. *New Woman, New Earth: Sexist Ideologies and Human Liberation.* New York: Harper & Row, 1978.

Sources on women in the church

Carroll, Jackson W., et al. *Women of the Cloth: New Opportunities for the Church.* New York: Harper & Row, 1983.

Lehman, Edward C., Jr., *Women Clergy: Breaking Through Gender Barriers.* New Brunswick, N.J.: Transaction Publications, 1985.

Parvey, Constance, ed. *The Community of Women and Men in the Church. Philadelphia: Fortress Press, 1983.*

Ruether, Rosemary Radford. *Women-Church.* New York: Harper & Row, 1986.

Sources on women and the Bible

Collins, Adela Yarbro, ed. *Feminist Perspectives in Biblical Scholarship.* Chico, Calif.: Scholars Press, 1985.

Exum, J. Cheryl, and Johanna W. H. Bos, eds. *Reasoning with the Foxes: Female Wit in a World of Male Power.* Decatur, Ga.: Scholars Press, 1988.

Fiorenza, Elisabeth Schüssler. *In Memory of Her: A Feminist Theological Reconstruction of Christian Origins.* New York: Crossroad, 1984.

Poethig, Eunice. *Good News Women.* Louisville, Ky.: Presbyterian Church (U.S.A.), 1987.

Probee, John S., and Bärbel von Wartgenberg Potter, eds. *New Eyes for Reading: Biblical and Theological Reflections by Women from the Third World.* Yorktown Heights, N.Y.: Meyer-Stone, 1986.

Robins, Wendy S., ed. *Through the Eyes of a Woman.* Rushden, England: World YWCA, 1986.

Russell, Letty M., ed. *Feminist Interpretation of the Bible.* Philadelphia: Westminster Press, 1985.

Stanton, Elizabeth Cady. *The Woman's Bible.* 1895. Reprint. Salem, N.H.: Ayer Co. Publications, 1972.

Tamez, Elsa, ed. *Through Her Eyes: Women's Theology from Latin America.* Maryknoll, N.Y.: Orbis Books, 1989.

Trible, Phyllis. *Texts of Terror: Literary-Feminist Readings of Biblical Narratives.* Philadelphia: Fortress Press, 1984.

Weems, Renita. *Just a Sister Away: A Womanist Vision of Women's Relationships in the Bible.* San Diego: LuraMedia, 1988.

Sources on feminist theology

Daly, Mary. *The Church and the Second Sex: Including the Feminist Postchristian.* New York: Harper & Row, 1968.

———. *Beyond God the Father: Toward a Philosophy of Women's Liberation.* Boston: Beacon Press, 1985.

Russell, Letty M. *The Future of Partnership.* Philadelphia: Westminster Press, 1979.

———. *Growth in Partnership.* Philadelphia: Westminster Press, 1981.

———. *The Liberating Word: A Guide to Nonsexist Interpretation of the Bible.* Philadelphia: Westminster Press, 1976.

Sources on feminist philosophy and theory

Daly, Mary. *Gyn/ecology: The Metaethics of Radical Feminism.* Boston: Beacon Press, 1978.

Johnson, Patricia Altenbernd, and Janet Kalven, eds. *With Both Eyes Open: Seeing Beyond Gender.* New York: Pilgrim Press, 1988.

Langland, Elizabeth, and Walter Gove, eds. *A Feminist Perspective in the Academy: The Difference It Makes.* Chicago: University of Chicago Press, 1983.

Rich, Adrienne. *Of Lies, Secrets and Silence: Selected Prose, 1966–1978.* New York: W. W. Norton & Co., 1979.

Chapter 4: Explorations in the Text

Sources on Judges 4:17–22

Boling, Robert G., tr. and ed. *Judges.* Anchor Bible. Garden City, N.Y.: Doubleday & Co., 1975.

Bos, Johanna W. H. "Out of the Shadows." In *Reasoning with the Foxes,* ed. Cheryl Exum and Johanna W. H. Bos. *Semeia* 42. Decatur, Ga.: Scholars Press, 1988.

Nicholson, E. W. "The Problem of צנח." In *Zeitschrift für die Alttestamentliche Wissenschaft* 89 (1977): 259–266.

Sources on 2 Kings 4:1–7

Brueggemann, Walter. *1 Kings.* Ed. John H. Hayes. Knox Preaching Guides. Atlanta: John Knox Press, 1983.

———. *2 Kings.* Ed. John J. Hayes. Knox Preaching Guides. Atlanta: John Knox Press, 1983.

———. *The Prophetic Imagination.* Philadelphia: Fortress Press, 1978.

Sources on Esther

Bos, Johanna W. H. *Ruth, Esther, Jonah.* Ed. John H. Hayes. Knox Preaching Guides. Atlanta: John Knox Press, 1986.

Moore, Carey A., ed. *Esther.* Anchor Bible. Garden City, N.Y.: Doubleday & Co., 1971.

For further reading

Belenky, Mary Field, et al. *Women's Ways of Knowing: The Development of Self, Voice, and Mind.* New York: Basic Books, 1986.

Ogletree, Thomas W. *Hospitality to the Stranger: Dimensions of Moral Understanding.* Philadelphia: Fortress Press, 1985.

Chapter 5: Reformed and Feminist

Sources on Ruth

Bos, Johanna W. H. *Ruth and Esther: Women in Alien Lands.* Nashville: Mission Education and Cultivation Program Department of the General Board of Global Ministries of The United Methodist Church, 1987.

Campbell, Edward F. *Ruth.* Anchor Bible. Garden City, N.Y.: Doubleday & Co. 1975.